# CORK
# BURNING

MICHAEL LENIHAN

# CORK BURNING

MERCIER PRESS

Comhairle Cathrach Chorcaí
Cork City Council

Plean Oidhreachta
CATHRACH CHORCAÍ

CORK CITY
Heritage Plan

An Chomhairle Oidhreachta
The Heritage Council

MERCIER PRESS
Cork
www.mercierpress.ie

© Michael Lenihan, 2018

ISBN: 978 1 78117 792 1

10 9 8 7 6 5 4 3 2 1

A CIP record for this title is available from the British Library

Printed and bound in the EU.

# CONTENTS

Acknowledgements 9

Introduction 11

Timeline of Events before the Burning of Cork City 19

Cork City before December 1920 25

The British Forces in Cork in 1920 51

Republican Cork 61

Arson Rampant in Cork 79

The Kilmichael Ambush 91

The Dillon's Cross Ambush 95

The Burning of the City 105

Business Premises Destroyed 145

Local Reaction to the Burning 157

British Reaction 171

Bishop Cohalan's Decree 179

Compensation Claims 183

Rebuilding Cork City 193

Epilogue 219

Appendix 1
The Higginson Enquiry 223

Appendix 2
The Strickland Enquiry 229

Bibliography 245

Index 251

To my grandson, Culann,
and granddaughter, Abigail.

Two of the temporary premises constructed shortly after the fire. (Author's collection)

# ACKNOWLEDGEMENTS

Finding images for *Cork Burning* was always going to be problematic, as they are extremely rare, and without the help and kindness of the following people this book would not have been possible: Pat Poland kindly lent me images from his collection on Cork firefighting; Fionnuala Mac Curtain gave me permission to use an image of her grandmother; Niall Murray sourced some of the images from the *Irish Examiner* archival collection, and John Dolan of the *Irish Examiner* provided assistance and kindly gave me permission to use same. A special word of thanks must go to Dan Breen of the Cork Public Museum for trawling through the museum's archives and providing me with some wonderful reports and images.

I would like also to thank Cork City Council and Niamh Twomey, Heritage Officer in the council, for their kind support and providing me with a heritage grant; David Grant, who kindly gave me permission to use information on his ADRIC website which proved invaluable; the staff of Cork City and County Archives and Cork City Library for their help; and Donal Ó Drisceoil and John Borgonovo of UCC, Diarmuid Ó Drisceoil, Antóin O'Callaghan, Ronnie Herlihy, Pat Poland, Tom Spalding and Jim Herlihy, whose interest and encouragement are always most welcome. Thanks to Louise Harrington for her wonderful insights into the firm of Chillingworth & Levie. And thanks to my good friends Noel Scannell and Martin Kelleher for providing additional information, and Denis, Tony and Anita Lenihan for their support.

A special word of thanks to the staff of Mercier Press, whose unwavering support produced this magnificent book, especially Alice Coleman for her expertise in designing the book; Wendy Logue, whose editorial help and expertise proved invaluable; Deirdre Roberts, whose marketing skills are crucial; and Mary Feehan, who took a personal interest in the book, and for her support in publishing this tome.

Last but not least I must thank my wife, Josephine, without whose help and tolerance this project would never have seen the light of day.

From 1907 motor cars were becoming a more familiar sight on Patrick Street, including ones like that seen in this photograph. Within ten years, Henry Ford had built a factory in Cork, on the Marina. (Author's collection)

# INTRODUCTION

On the night of 11–12 December 1920, Cork city would suffer almost unprecedented destruction at the hands of British forces intent on revenge for the death of their comrades in Irish Republican Army (IRA) ambushes at Kilmichael and Dillon's Cross. Not since the events of the 1916 Rising in Dublin had such scenes of mass destruction been witnessed in Ireland.

Cork itself had played little part in the Rising, largely due to the orders published and dispatched by Eoin MacNeill, the head of the Irish Volunteers, calling off the manoeuvres which were to be a cover for the beginning of the action. However, in the years that followed, and particularly during the War of Independence, Cork city and county became one of the most active and violent areas in all of Ireland. The city would witness great savagery on both sides, and the murder of the first Republican lord mayor, Tomás MacCurtain, and the hunger strike of his successor, Terence MacSwiney, would bring international media attention to the city, much to the embarrassment of the British government.

On the British side, two forces – the Black and Tans and the Auxiliaries – were the perpetrators of much of the violence that both city and county would suffer during 1920 and 1921. Winston Churchill, the British secretary of state for war and no friend to Ireland, had begun recruiting the Black and Tans to reinforce the depleted Royal Irish Constabulary (RIC) in early 1920. In May 1920 Churchill's friend Major General Henry Hugh Tudor was appointed as police advisor to the viceroy; he was later promoted to chief of police. Tudor's intention was 'to take the war to the IRA and make Ireland an appropriate hell for those rebels whose trade is violence'. July 1920 saw another recruitment initiative, this time for the Auxiliary Division, which became, if anything, even more ruthless than the Black and Tans.

These new forces were to strike terror into the inhabitants of the country with the aim of diffusing support for the IRA. Looking at the events preceding the destruction of Cork city, murder, incendiary attacks, raids, theft, looting and intimidation were all part of their terror tactics. The destruction of premises particularly associated with republicanism, such as the Sinn Féin and Gaelic Athletic Association (GAA) clubs, happened increasingly frequently as the war wore on. British Prime Minister David Lloyd George actively encouraged this policy of attrition and on 9 November 1920 declared, 'We have murder by the throat!'

Less than three weeks later an event would occur that would completely undermine Lloyd George's statement. On 28 November, led by Tom Barry, a unit of the West Cork IRA carried out a successful ambush on a large Auxiliary force at Kilmichael, which left all but one of the Auxiliaries dead. Unfortunately Cork city was to pay an enormous price for this ambush. In the days following Kilmichael major arson attacks took place on several buildings in the city. The Thomas Ashe Sinn Féin Club, the headquarters of the Irish Transport and General Workers' Union (ITGWU), Dalton's restaurant and O'Gorman's drapery shop were among those destroyed, and City Hall, seen as a political hotbed of nationalism and already the target of several arson attempts as early as July 1920, was also damaged.

But this was simply the precursor to the main event. Following another successful IRA ambush on 11 December at Dillon's Cross, the reaction of the crown forces was to bring the terror campaign to a new level. The principal business premises in the city were selected for destruction amidst an orgy of looting. It is clear from the progression of the arson attacks across the city that these were designed to cause the maximum harm to businesses and to have the greatest impact possible on its citizens. Unfortunately, the structural layout of Patrick Street and the narrowness of the streets intersecting the burning buildings allowed the rapid spread of fires which facilitated the total devastation of one complete side of the main thoroughfare of the city. Luckily, firemen under the able command of Captain Alfred Hutson managed to prevent the spread of fire to the English Market and other buildings at the end of Patrick Street and to the intersecting lanes extending to Grand Parade and Georges Street, but the intense heat from the burning buildings blistered the paint on the buildings on the opposite side of the street. That some of the premises destroyed were owned by people with unionist sympathies made no difference to the Auxiliaries in their quest for revenge.

The deliberate destruction of the most valuable business premises maximised unemployment and homelessness in the city in the days and months that followed. Millions of pounds' worth of damage was caused and some businesses never reopened following the fire.

In the immediate aftermath, the British government's reaction was to try to deny that the event took place. This was quickly followed by an attempt to blame Republicans for burning down their own city. The government's next course of action was to establish a military investigation into its own armed forces. A story was then concocted blaming a spark from City Hall, which had conveniently moved location to near Patrick Street, for the burning of the entire city. The bishop of Cork, Daniel Cohalan, then became involved, issuing a decree of excommunication on members of the IRA involved in any ambush. The members of Cork Corporation took issue with Bishop Cohalan, questioning where his sympathies lay – not with the emotionally distressed Cork citizens and their burned-out city, it seemed.

With commercial insurance largely covering stock only, the British government finally agreed to pay compensation, but continually attempted to whittle down the awards claimed. The Civil War further exacerbated delays on payment, with many fearing the city would be burned once again by evacuating anti-Treaty forces. Another source of conflict was the proposition by Cork Corporation to widen some streets and close others. The issue of whether Cork labour and materials should be used became a cause of disagreement between shop owners and unions. In the end it took seven years for the final building in the reconstruction to be completed.

Following the Cork burnings, photographs of the scenes of destruction proved to be a very powerful instrument against the British government's terror campaign in Ireland. It was particularly embarrassing for the British government that these images were so reminiscent of the many towns and villages destroyed by German artillery just a few years previously during the First World War. My own interest was initially piqued by a series of commercial postcards published in the aftermath of the devastation. These original images were all press photographs, some taken for *The Manchester Guardian*, which were republished by the Cork printing firm of

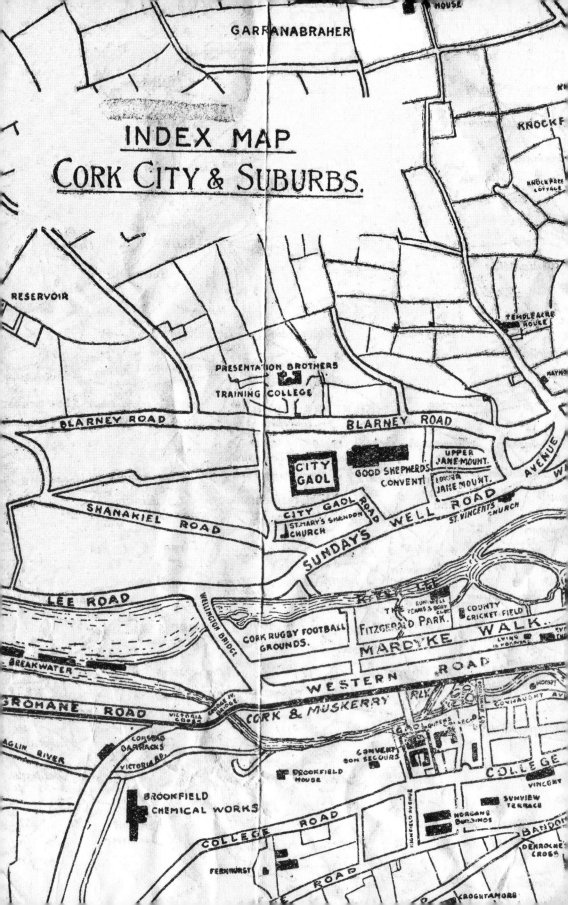

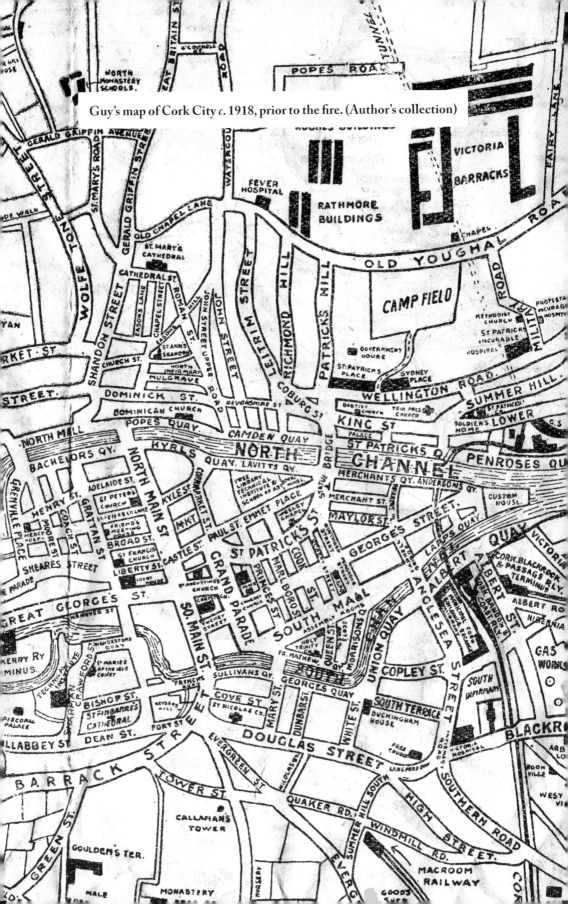

Guy's map of Cork City *c.* 1918, prior to the fire. (Author's collection)

Members of the RIC outside a shop on Patrick Street *c.* 1920–21. The RIC suffered many resignations during this time, causing reinforcements in the shape of the Black and Tans and Auxiliaries to be sent to Ireland in 1920. (Courtesy of the National Library of Ireland)

Guy & Co. based on Patrick Street. Twelve cards in total were published. Although surviving copies are extremely rare, I succeeded in purchasing all twelve original postcards over many years.

As time went by I became more and more interested in the subject, but I soon discovered that little had been published on the subject at the time. There was the Irish Labour Party's report of January 1921, *Who Burnt Cork City?*, which consisted of over seventy eyewitness reports recorded immediately after the burning and was considered the seminal work. However, no further books were published immediately after the catastrophe and, over time, interest in the story of the burning of Cork city appears to have waned.

# INTRODUCTION

The aim of this book is to gather together original sources, particularly images, to provide a pictorial record of the city before, during and after the burning. The nucleus of this book is my own photographic collection, enhanced by the archives of *The Cork Examiner* (today's *Irish Examiner*), Mercier Press and Cork Public Museum, as well as images from Pat Poland's collection, Cork City Library and Cork City and County Archives. These contemporary illustrations still provoke the question asked at the time – how could an army of occupation destroy a city it was supposed to be protecting? Some eyewitness accounts taken from the Irish Labour Party's report are used in conjunction with the images of the burning to convey an authentic representation of what it was like to actually experience these events.

While working on this book, one thing that struck me over and over was the resilience displayed by the citizens of Cork city, as businesses struggled to reopen in temporary premises under the most horrific of conditions. The rebuilding of the city centre and, subsequently, City Hall, is a remarkable testimony to their spirit in the face of such adversity and makes me proud to be a native of this great city.

The face of the clock on Cork City Hall with bullet holes where it had been fired at by British forces. (Courtesy of Mercier Archive)

# TIMELINE OF EVENTS BEFORE
# THE BURNING OF CORK CITY

## 1919

18 November: IRA raids Murray's gun shop on Patrick Street for guns and ammunition.

## 1920

January: Recruitment starts for a new force to strengthen the RIC. It becomes known as the Black and Tans.

31 January: Tomás MacCurtain, commanding officer, Cork No. 1 Brigade, IRA, is elected lord mayor.

17 February: IRA attack RIC dispatch party near Union Quay Barracks.

11 March: RIC District Inspector McDonagh shot on Pope's Quay and seriously wounded. RIC Constable Timothy Scully shot dead at Glanmire.

14 March: Bishop Cohalan denounces the Volunteers from the pulpit, declaring that a campaign against the police is a campaign against public order.

19 March: Shooting of RIC Constable Murtagh at Pope's Quay, Cork.

20 March: Tomás MacCurtain murdered in front of his wife and family at his home on Thomas Davis Street by members of the RIC.

25 March: Black and Tans arrive in Ireland. Cork headquarters are at Empress Place, Summerhill.

31 March: Terence MacSwiney elected lord mayor of Cork.

5 April: Burning of income tax offices on the South Mall and South Terrace. Burning of RIC barracks at Togher, Cork.

12 May: Burning of RIC barracks at Commons Road, Cork.

23 June: First members of the Auxiliary Division arrive in Ireland.

24 June: Burning of RIC barracks at Blackrock, Cork.

2 July: Military vehicle from Victoria Barracks hijacked at the GSWR railway station.

12 July: Burning of three RIC barracks at King Street, St Luke's and Lower Glanmire Road, Cork.

15 July: Two British Army lorries captured and burned at Dennehy's Cross, Cork.

17 July: RIC Divisional Commissioner G. Brice Ferguson Smyth shot dead at the County Club, South Mall.

11 August: Republican prisoners in Cork Gaol begin hunger strike.

12 August: City Hall raided by military, Terence MacSwiney arrested and immediately begins hunger strike.

22 August: RIC District Inspector Swanzy shot dead by members of Cork's IRA in retaliation for the murder of Tomás MacCurtain.

24 September: Attempt to kidnap General Strickland at King Street fails.

27 September: Bomb explosion at Castle & Co. shop near the Cork Arcade. Ten other buildings nearby sustain serious structural damage.

3 October: Shooting of RIC Constable Chave on Patrick Street, Cork.

8 October: Auxiliary shot dead and another wounded in an attack in the city centre. Auxiliary shot dead and another three wounded in an attack on a military lorry at Barrack Street, Cork.

9 October: Cork City Hall set on fire.

25 October: Terence MacSwiney and Joseph Murphy both die after more than seventy days on hunger strike.

18 November: RIC Sergeant J. O'Donoghue shot dead at White Street, Cork.

21 November: Three civilians shot dead by Black and Tans at Broad Lane and North Mall, Cork. A week-long spate of bomb and arson attacks by the anti-Sinn Féin Society begins in Cork city centre. In the early hours of the morning Dwyer & Co., Washington Street, is set alight, causing £10,000 damage. Dwyer & Co. is later awarded £2,592 in compensation.

22 November: K Company of the Auxiliary Division formed by Brigadier General Frank Percy Crozier. The company commander is Colonel Owen W. R. G. Latimer.

23 November: Sinn Féin Club on Watercourse Road destroyed by fire.

**The old City Hall, constructed to house the first Cork Exhibition of 1852. (Courtesy of Mercier Archive)**

24 November: Brian Boru Piper's Club and Sinn Féin Club, Hardwick Street, destroyed.

25 November: No. 56 Grand Parade, which houses the Artane Clothing Co. and the Sinn Féin headquarters, burned.

27 November: Sinn Féin offices at 53 North Main Street destroyed. St Michael's GAA Club, Blackrock, and St Columba's Hall Recreation Club burned. Forrest & Sons at the corner of Cook Street set ablaze and nine people living overhead have to be rescued.

28 November: Roche's jewellers, Egan's jewellers and John Teape jewellers on Patrick Street looted. Cahill & Co., Blackthorn House and the American Shoe Co. are set on fire. Only the American Shoe Co. survives. The Kilmichael ambush results in the deaths of seventeen Auxiliaries.

29 November: ITGWU offices on Camden Quay set on fire and firemen fired on to prevent them from extinguishing the flames.

30 November: Thomas Ashe Sinn Féin Club on Fr Mathew Quay destroyed. Cork City Hall set on fire but the blaze is extinguished. Egan's jewellers set alight and firemen threatened at gunpoint, but the fire is put out.

1 December: O'Gorman's drapery shop and Dalton's restaurant on King Street destroyed by fire. American Shoe Co. set alight again and this time destroyed.

2 December: Offices of Irish National Insurance Co., Marlboro Street, destroyed. Remains of the Auxiliaries killed during the Kilmichael ambush paraded through Patrick Street, increasing tension within the city.

10 December: Martial Law introduced in Counties Cork, Kerry, Limerick and Tipperary.

11 December: Dillon's Cross ambush: Auxiliaries are fired on and grenades thrown into their Crossley tenders, wounding thirteen, one of whom subsequently dies. Six houses burned at Dillon's Cross and Jeremiah and Cornelius Delany murdered in front of their family.

A busy scene on Patrick Street *c.* 1915. Forrest & Sons, a high-class costumers is located at 33 and 34 Patrick Street on the corner of Cook Street, opposite the Victoria Hotel. (Author's collection)

# CORK CITY BEFORE
# DECEMBER 1920

In the late nineteenth century many people in Cork lived in houses unfit for human habitation. Countless numbers lived in low rent, substandard dwellings and rarely had enough food, heat or clothes. However, by the end of Queen Victoria's reign, significant improvements had been made in the physical environment of the city. Living standards had improved generally and mortality had fallen considerably. Cork Corporation began to build a series of workmen's cottages, which were completed by 1908 – Barrett's Buildings, followed by Roche's and Sutton's buildings, had been constructed on the north side of the city. These new housing schemes were built on the outskirts of the city as it was thought that building in the centre of the city would perpetuate slums. In 1870 the death rate in Cork had been a staggering 152 per 1,000 births. By 1917, due to public health initiatives, it had fallen below 100 deaths per 1,000 births.

Despite the corporation's work, the shortage of proper housing continued to be a major factor well into the twentieth century, impinging on the poorer and less well-off sections of Cork society. From 1859 to 1919 the local authorities built only 700 houses. This resulted in the continued existence of tenements, where the poor rented rooms in large old houses that had been vacated by Cork's elite classes, who had moved to more desirable homes in the suburbs. These tenements housed large families, who shared an outside toilet with no washing facilities for personal hygiene beyond an external cold-water tap. Just two years before the First World War, the chief medical officer of the corporation reported that 3,102 houses were necessary to solve the problem of overcrowding, disease and poor hygiene. By the

**An advertisement for Forrest & Sons. (Author's collection)**

end of the war, *The Cork Examiner* was reporting that many children were living in extreme poverty and facing 'the day's school-work breakfast-less'. Exacerbating the poverty was the fact that women were treated as second-class citizens, without the right to vote and earning only 50 to 60 per cent of what men doing the same job were getting.

Society at this time was marked by a huge degree of inequality between the richest and poorest. The upper 1 per cent owned 70 per cent of the total wealth, and the top 10 per cent owned around 90 per cent of the total wealth. £160 per year was the annual income at which income tax became payable and this was considered to be the dividing line between the working and middle classes.

The average working week in 1912 was fifty-six hours. A skilled man in regular work earning £100 per year could probably bring up a family without too much strain. A crewman on a ship like the *Titanic* could have expected to earn around that amount per year, provided he was in good health and kept up regular employment. However, many were forced to survive on less. It is not surprising, therefore, that trade union membership grew rapidly between 1900 and 1913. In 1913, during the Dublin Lockout, 20,000 workers were on strike.

Times were even more difficult for the unemployed. In the worst cases of hardship, the only form of assistance was private charities and the Poor Law. A foretaste of the welfare state arrived in 1908, with the introduction of the old age pension, calculated at five shillings per week for those over sixty-nine. Following this, the National Insurance Act of 1911 provided health and unemployment benefit, calculated at ten shillings per week for contributors who became ill. Significantly, it did not cover the insured's dependants, nor was any provision made for the uninsured or the long-term jobless.

**On the right of this picture is Cash's department store. The name was an amalgamation of parts of the owners' names: Carmichael, Arnott and McOstrich. Note the beautiful gas lamps outside, which were a feature of Patrick Street for many years. (Author's collection)**

*Above:*

Trams and hackneys vie for trade on Patrick Street *c.* 1918. These were the main means of transport for the general public in the early twentieth century. (Author's collection)

*Opposite top:*

This wonderful sketch of Cash & Co., which had the finest shop frontage on the street, comes from the late nineteenth century. (Author's collection)

*Opposite bottom:*

The Union Jack flag (seen to the right) hung from some Patrick Street premises as proprietors demonstrated their allegiance to Britain. (Author's collection)

**A wonderful view of the old premises of The Munster**

In 1920 a Dominican priest, Father A. McSweeney, published a survey on poverty in the city. He reported that a wage below twenty-one shillings per week (about €1.35 in today's money) placed people in poverty and that many people were earning less than nineteen shillings (€1.20) per week and lived in chronic want. His report concentrated on working-class families, not those even less fortunate who were out of work and living in destitution. Their only recourse was outdoor relief, a small allowance to prevent them from entering the workhouse.

Despite the poverty and inequality, this was not a time without optimism. In the Cork city survey of 1926 it was recorded that people believed they were better off than the previous generation and that their children would be better off than they were. The hope was that new industries associated with electricity, auto-manufacture and chemicals would soon offer cleaner and more reliable work.

Even with the improvements in the infrastructure of the city and the building of the corporation houses, in 1920 Cork was still a small, compact city made up of a disproportionate number of small lanes and alleys where the city's poorer inhabitants eked out a living as best they could. The wealthier inhabitants were able to live in suburbs such as Sundays Well, Douglas, Tivoli and Blackrock, which were well designed and did not need the improvements which the inner city did. Many of the city's more prosperous establishments, such as banks and doctors' surgeries, had their professionals living upstairs. In the large department stores, such as Cash's and The Munster Arcade, their apprentices lived above, in cramped, unhealthy conditions. Based on the figures from the 1911 census, the population of the city would have been around 80,000. Catholics were in the majority at a staggering 88.5 per cent, with the remainder largely members of the Church of Ireland, who made up 10 per cent of the population.

Then, as now, the main thoroughfare of the city was Patrick Street. The first development of Patrick Street occurred in 1783 and the name first appeared in *The Cork Evening Post* on 22 May that year. Newspapers and street directories from the time of the burning show that many of the premises on the street had very long trading traditions. Some of the first known buildings on the street were Reidy's Le Chateau, built in 1793; T. W. Murray's Sports Shop, built in 1828; and Day's, which was established in 1831 at No. 103 Patrick Street. The Victoria Hotel was built

# The LONDON HOUSE Ltd.,

## 14 & 15, PATRICK STREET, CORK.

Irish Bog Oak a Speciality.

Glass & China Department.    Toy & Fancy Basket Ware Rooms.    Hosiers, Glovers, Furriers.
Ladies' Outfitters.    Irish Lace.    Travelling Requisites, Trunks, Rugs, Dress Baskets.
Telephone 362.

**An advertisement for The London House Ltd in the 1918 *Guy's Directory*, showing a very rare internal view of this department store. (Author's collection)**

in 1810 and was the city's oldest until it closed in 2014. The famous clockmakers, Mangan's, was established at No. 3 Patrick Street in 1817. Sir John Arnott had a store there in 1842, which later became Alexander Grant's department store. The Munster Arcade opened in 1866. Later famous names include Carmichael's, established in 1868; Egan's, opened in 1870 (but established in the 1780s on Castle Street); Purcell's printers, established in 1834; and Guy's printers, which had premises on Patrick Street in 1842. Fitzgerald's menswear has been on the street since 1860, although it has moved several times.

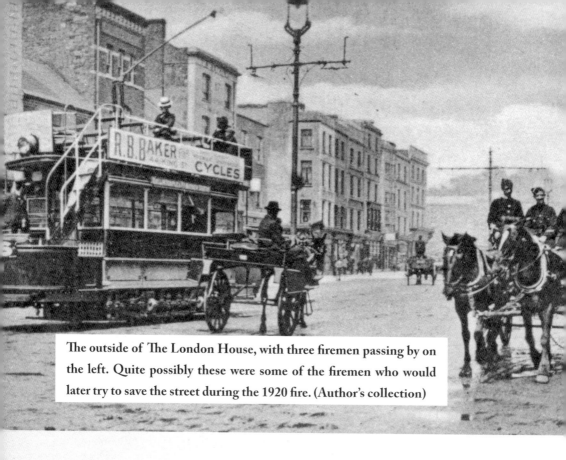

The outside of The London House, with three firemen passing by on the left. Quite possibly these were some of the firemen who would later try to save the street during the 1920 fire. (Author's collection)

One of the landmarks of today's Patrick Street is the Roches Stores building, but the spring of 1919 saw that famous department store taking up residence in the Allman's building on the corner of Winthrop Street and Patrick Street, next door to Cash & Co. In *The Story of Roches Stores*, Patrick Fitzgerald, the store's manager, is recorded as saying:

Our opening sale here surpassed all our expectations and its spontaneous success no doubt had its place in Mr Roche's decision to later purchase the 'London House'. Allman's reputation for quality goods and the method of advertising the 'Transfer Sale' brought the people in such numbers that they had to be regulated and only allowed in in batches; in short we were overwhelmed and continued so for such a period. … In the short time allotted to get ready for the sale we found ourselves on the eve of the event without the windows being dressed and scarcely knew what to do about it. Mr Roche solved the problem by ordering a full-sized poster for the windows which ran: 'Too busy to dress the windows, come inside'.

Clearly this solved the window-dressing issue and people 'fought to get inside'.

Mr Roche had purchased Allman's only a few months previous to the opening and ran it very successfully whilst he was negotiating for The London House. On acquiring the latter in June 1919, he disposed of the Allman's premises, transferring the business and staff to The London House. The London House had already existed for fifty years on Patrick Street. Acquiring it had been a stressful business and stretched William Roche's finances to the limit, but the new shop became so successful that it increased its trade five-fold. In September the name of the shop was changed by legal resolution to Roches Stores Ltd.

When Roche sold Allman's it was converted into the Lee Cinema. Unfortunately for the new owners, within six weeks of opening the cinema would be burned to the ground. Despite this it would later be rebuilt and the building is still a feature of today's Patrick Street.

Many of the buildings on Patrick Street had varied forms of architecture and the canopies outside these shop fronts lend an almost continental air to the street. (Author's collection)

*Below left:*

**William Roche and James Keating initially started their operation, the Cork Furniture Stores, on Merchant Street (which existed between 11 and 12 Patrick Street, the current location of Debenhams), where they had a shop and seven warehouses. (Author's collection)**

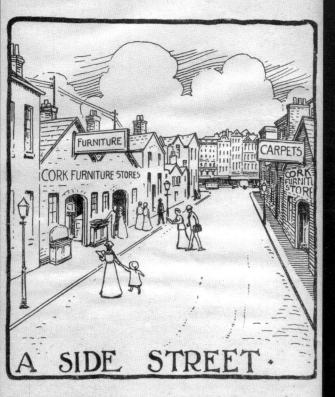

ONE OF THE STORES.

A SIDE STREET.

THIS is a view of one of the Stores. We have seven of these Stores, all of them crammed with Furniture, and, being situated in a Side Street, under low rents, enables the Furniture Stores to

Sell below all Front Shops.

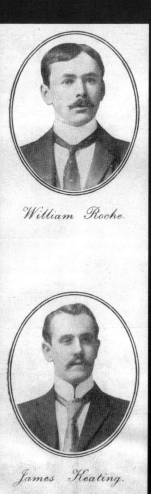

*William Roche.*

*James Keating.*

*Above:*

**William Roche and James Keating, the two partners who founded the Cork Furniture Stores, the precursor to Roches Stores. (Author's collection)**

A receipt from F. Allman & Co., hosiers, glovers and shirtmakers, before the premises was taken over by Roches Stores. (Author's collection)

This view of Cash's gives us a good indication of the sheer size of the building. The second storey was where the live-in apprentices were housed. (Author's collection)

William Egan, proprietor of Egan's high-class jewellery, watch-making, gold and silver workshops, c. 1908. His ancestors had operated a jewellery shop in Castle Street from the 1780s. (Author's collection)

The wonderful window display of William Egan & Sons at 32 Patrick Street. Egan's was renowned as the city's finest silversmiths. (Author's collection)

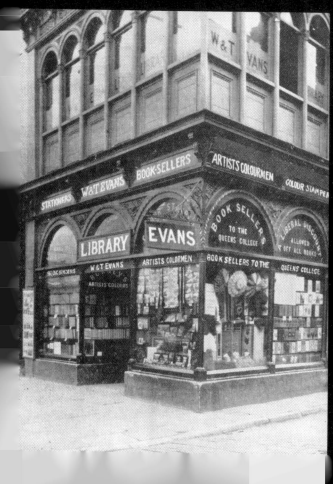

# W. & T. EVANS

BEG to call the attention of Heads of Colleges and Students to their great facilities for supplying, at the shortest notice, all Books required for the INTERMEDIATE, UNIVERSITY, CIVIL SERVICE, and other Examinations. They endeavour to have always in stock every work of any importance, and will procure at once any that happen not to be in stock on receipt of order.

They invite correspondence about the supplying of College and School Books, and will be happy to furnish quotations and catalogues, etc., by return post.

## 11, ST. PATRICK STREET,,
### ❋ CORK. ❋

*Booksellers to the University College and to the Intermediate Board.*

*Left:*
An advertisement from Evans' bookshop. They were clearly proud to be booksellers to University College Cork. (Author's collection)

*Below:*
A recruiting scene from 1914. Just six years later, the shutters of Mangan's clockmakers and jewellers would be torn down and the shop looted by Auxiliaries and Black and Tans. (Courtesy of the *Irish Examiner*)

An extremely rare view of the partially constructed National Monument at the time of King Edward's visit to the Greater Cork International Exhibition in 1903. The RIC constables on horseback represent a direct contrast to the undercurrent of republicanism being commemorated by the building of the monument. (Lenihan Collection, courtesy of Cork Public Museum)

*Left:*

A rare view of the interior of The Munster Arcade, where huge stocks of drapery were stored. (Author's collection)

*Right:*

The Munster Arcade was one of Cork's premier department stores and a contractor to the military and navy before its demise. (Author's collection)

All of the shops to the right of this Patrick Street scene survived the fire, suffering little more than blistered paint caused by the intense heat from the fires on the other side of the street. (Author's collection)

*Above:*

A rare image of the premises of Alexander Grant & Co. on Patrick Street. (Courtesy of Cork Public Museum)

*Below:*

An advertisement for Alexander Grant & Co., which claimed to have the largest stock of Irish manufactured drapery goods in the south of Ireland. (Author's collection)

# ALEXANDER GRANT & CO.
## CORK.

*CONVENT AND SEMINARY OUTFITS.* ✍ *STUDENTS' OUTFITS.*

*At Moderate Prices.*

We hold the Largest Stock of Irish Manufactured Drapery Goods in the South of Ireland.

# PATRICK STREET & GRAND PARADE.

Grant & Co., which extended from Patrick Street to the Grand Parade, was the first building to be set on fire on the night of 11 December 1920. This image shows the Grand Parade entrance. (Author's collection)

Cork's oldest hotel, the Victoria Hotel, survived the fire, even though Forrest's, to the immediate left on the other side of Cook Street, was destroyed. (Author's collection)

An image of the City Hall and the Carnegie Free Library, *c.* 1912, with Parnell Bridge in the foreground. (Author's collection)

Major General Sir Henry Tudor at an RIC parade in Dublin. (Courtesy of Mercier Archive)

# THE BRITISH FORCES IN CORK

# IN 1920

The date generally accepted as the start of the War of Independence in Ireland is 21 January 1919, when two significant events took place. The first of these was an attack led by Dan Breen and Seán Treacy on a shipment of gelignite being transported to a quarry at Soloheadbeg, Tipperary, during which two members of the RIC were shot dead. The second was the first meeting of Dáil Éireann, the newly formed Irish government, which had been set up as a result of the overwhelming vote for Sinn Féin during the 1918 general election.

When the war broke out, the British forces on the island consisted of the army and the RIC, with the latter composed largely of Irishmen. The British military in Cork had been based since 1806 in what was initially called New Barracks, then Cork Barracks and finally, after the death of Queen Victoria, Victoria Barracks (the name changed to Collins Barracks after independence). The garrison was stationed there to defend the city in the event of an invasion and to help the civil authorities maintain control of the city and its surrounding areas. During the 1916 Rising, it was the military who surrounded the Cork Volunteers in their hall in Sheares Street, forcing a stand-off that led to the Volunteers standing down and surrendering their weapons. By 1919 the 6th Infantry Division, commanded by General Peter Strickland, and the 17th Infantry Brigade were based in the barracks.

However, at the start of the War of Independence the IRA was well aware that it was the RIC, with its local knowledge, and not the military, which posed the greatest threat to its men, so it specifically targeted policemen and RIC barracks in its attacks. As time went on, with the RIC being forced to withdraw its forces into

large towns, and increasing numbers of RIC men resigning and being killed, the British decided to bolster the police force with two new reserves.

The Black and Tans, officially known as the Royal Irish Constabulary Special Reserve, consisted of temporary constables recruited in Great Britain from early 1920, the majority of whom were veterans of the First World War. The first of these recruits arrived in Ireland on 25 March 1920, only to find that there was a shortage of RIC uniforms. Instead they were issued with khaki army uniforms and surplus RIC tunics, caps and belts. The nickname 'Black and Tans' was taken from the colours of these improvised uniforms, as they reminded people of a famous pack of hunting dogs with that name.

These new temporary constables were paid the relatively high wage of 10 shillings a day, as well as being given full board and lodging. With minimal police training, their main role was to act as reinforcements to the RIC. As they were not subject to the strict military discipline they would have been used to, they often indulged

Victoria Barracks, the headquarters of British military rule in Cork, also housed the majority of the Auxiliaries and Black and Tans. (Author's collection)

in arbitrary reprisals and quickly became infamous for their attacks on civilians and property. From the summer of 1920 the Black and Tans burned and sacked many small towns and villages in Ireland, beginning with Tuam in County Galway and including Trim, Balbriggan, Knockcrogherty, Thurles and Templemore according to the report of the American Commission on Conditions in Ireland, published in 1921.

The Auxiliary Division of the Royal Irish Constabulary (ADRIC), generally known simply as the Auxiliaries or Auxies, was a paramilitary unit of the RIC commanded by Brigadier General Frank Percy Crozier. Set up in July 1920 and comprising mainly former British Army officers, its role was to conduct counter-insurgency operations against the IRA. The Auxiliaries were divided into companies, each about 100 strong, heavily armed and highly mobile. They wore either RIC uniforms or their old army uniforms with appropriate police badges, along with distinctive tam o' shanter caps. As the two groups often worked in unison, the Auxiliaries were sometimes confused with the Black and Tans and on occasion the

The Cork Volunteers, renamed the IRA in 1919 following the establishment of Dáil Éireann, parade through Great Georges Street in early 1916. Great Georges Street was renamed Washington Street by the Republican-led Cork Corporation in 1918. (Author's collection)

An armed RIC patrol blocks access to part of Patrick Street. Note the Brooke Hughes photographic studio above The Munster Arcade, which was destroyed on 11 December. (Courtesy of the *Irish Examiner*)

latter name was used to cover both groups. Many of the crimes attributed to the Black and Tans were actually the work of the Auxiliaries.

This elite, ex-officer division proved to be much more effective than the Black and Tans, especially in the key area of gathering intelligence, but many did not cope well with the frustrations of counter-insurgency work. Hurriedly recruited, poorly trained and with an ill-defined role, they soon gained an ugly reputation for drunkenness, lack of discipline and brutality worse than that of the Black and Tans. This led to them being nicknamed Tudor's Toughs after Major General Sir Henry Hugh Tudor, who was police advisor to Dublin Castle and then chief of police from 1920 until the end of the war. Tudor justified the assaults perpetrated by the Auxiliaries by arguing that it would have taken too long to reinforce the RIC with trained recruits. His new Auxiliary force was to be strictly temporary: its members, known as temporary cadets, enlisted for a year and, according to Ernest McCall's book *Tudor's Toughs*, their pay was £7 per week (twice what a constable was paid), plus a sergeant's allowance.

The Auxiliaries were generally disliked by the RIC, who considered them too brutal, and they seem to have been unpopular with the British Army as well. One

British officer, who served as adjutant for the 2nd Battalion, Cameron Highlanders, wrote in his memoirs that the Auxiliaries were totally undisciplined by regimental standards. As the campaign against the IRA and Sinn Féin members was stepped up and police reprisals increased following IRA attacks, they became infamous for their reprisals on civilians and the burning of houses, shops and creameries, one of their main weapons of terror.

One of the most notorious of the Auxiliary companies, K Company, was formed by Brigadier General Crozier on 22 November 1920. It consisted of three platoons drawn from other Auxiliary companies and was commanded by Lieutenant Colonel Owen W. R. G. Latimer. By December this company was stationed in Victoria Barracks in Cork, although due to a shortage of accommodation at the barracks, Latimer was billeted in the Imperial Hotel. The company strength was sixty-seven in all. It was the ambush of two truckloads of K Company at Dillon's Cross on 11 December 1920 that led to the infamous events in Cork city that night, events in which both the Auxiliaries and the Black and Tans would play a major role.

**Auxiliaries search passengers alighting from a train at Glanmire (now Kent) Station. (Courtesy of Mercier Archive)**

Members of the notorious K Company, formed in November 1920, who were the main perpetrators of the burning of Cork city. (Courtesy of Mercier Archive)

*Left:*
Brigadier General Crozier, commander of the Auxiliary Division. (Courtesy of Mercier Archive)

*Below:*
One of the Auxiliaries' methods of terror was to burn premises in reprisal for attacks. In this picture the Auxiliary on the left is holding a petrol can. (Courtesy of Mercier Archive)

A group of Auxiliaries at Union Quay RIC Barracks wearing assorted uniforms. They had no particular type of uniform and, like the Black and Tans, it often consisted of a combination of RIC tunics and khaki trousers, and even civilian trench coats. (Courtesy of Mercier Archive)

Tomás MacCurtain. (Courtesy of Mercier Archive)

# REPUBLICAN CORK

Long known as the 'Rebel City', it is perhaps not surprising that a Cork City Corps of Irish Volunteers was founded in December 1913, just weeks after the official foundation of the organisation in Dublin. Slowly but surely the movement grew until eventually the Volunteers were openly carrying out drills in the Cork Cornmarket yard. By the time of the Easter Rising 1916 there were forty-seven companies of Volunteers throughout the county, although Eoin MacNeill's countermand orders caused such confusion that the Cork Volunteers largely failed to act during the Rising. In the city itself, men from different companies who had come from country areas were staying in the Volunteer Hall, primed for action, where they were joined by the city Volunteers. But with the failure to land arms from the *Aud*, they remained poorly armed, and with no clear instructions forthcoming from the command in Dublin, no definitive action was taken. The British military command in Cork quickly declared that unless the Volunteers in the hall disarmed and surrendered, the city would be shelled. To prevent bloodshed, Dr Cohalan, the bishop of Cork, offered to broker a deal. On 28 April the Volunteers, recognising their weak position, handed over their arms to the lord mayor – it had been agreed that these would be returned to them at a later date, but the British later reneged on the deal. In the days following, many republicans in the city, as in the rest of the country, were rounded up and incarcerated in various prisons in England and Frongoch Internment Camp in Wales until a general amnesty was granted.

In contrast to the inaction of 1916, during the War of Independence the Cork brigades of the IRA proved themselves to be some of the most effective guerrilla fighters in the country and their actions provoked the British forces based in the city and county into increasingly violent reprisals. These reprisals included a number of arson attacks in Cork city, which culminated in the destruction of 1920, but earlier that year two events took place which would escalate tensions between the IRA and the British forces in the city to breaking point – the assassination of the city's lord mayor, Tomás MacCurtain, who was also the commanding officer of Cork No. 1 Brigade of the IRA, and the arrest and death of his successor, Terence MacSwiney.

## THE ASSASSINATION OF TOMÁS MacCURTAIN

Tomás MacCurtain, the youngest of a family of twelve, was born at Ballyknockane, County Cork, in March 1884. Educated at Burnford National School, and later at the North Monastery, Cork, he joined the Irish Republican Brotherhood in 1907 and was one of the founders of the Cork Volunteers in December 1913. He was also a member of the Gaelic League, which promoted Irish culture and the Irish language, and it was at a League meeting that he first encountered Elizabeth Walsh (Eibhlís Breathnach), whom he married on 28 June 1908.

In early May 1916, following the events of the Easter Rising, MacCurtain was arrested along with other known Cork republicans and was imprisoned in Wakefield Jail, Frongoch Internment Camp and then Reading Jail. When he was released in December 1916, he returned to Cork and was soon heavily involved in the reorganisation of the Cork Volunteers, but the leaders of that organisation were by then marked men. In January 1919 the Cork Brigade was reorganised and MacCurtain became brigade commandant of Cork No. 1 Brigade, which covered the city and mid Cork, a position he would retain until his death.

At the start of 1920 MacCurtain was elected to Cork Corporation and shortly thereafter, on 31 January, was elected lord mayor of Cork, the first openly republican lord mayor to hold this office. At the same time he was still the commandant of Cork No. 1 Brigade, and on 19 March he called to brigade headquarters at the shop of Sheila and Nora Wallace in St Augustine Street to meet some of his officers. Tadhg Barry, a founding member and officer of the Cork Volunteers, left Wallace's with him. MacCurtain was on his way home to Thomas Davis Street, Blackpool, accompanied by his brother-in-law, James Walsh, when he heard about the shooting by the IRA of an RIC constable named Joseph Murtagh on Pope's Quay at around 11 p.m. that evening. Once home, MacCurtain spent time on the phone with the North Infirmary and when he discovered that the constable was dead, he made sure to contact the family and pass on his condolences. He went to bed after midnight. Also in the house that evening were his wife, Elizabeth, and their five children, the youngest of whom was only ten months old, as well as Elizabeth's brother, three sisters, two nieces, a nephew and her mother, who was an invalid.

Some time between 12.10 a.m. and 1.15 a.m. on Saturday 20 March, MacCurtain's thirty-sixth birthday, armed men with blackened faces surrounded the house. They banged on the door until it was opened by Elizabeth. While she was held at the door, two men rushed upstairs and shot the lord mayor, fatally wounding him. He died shortly afterwards.

**An aerial view of the funeral of Tomás MacCurtain showing the enormous crowds who attended. (Courtesy of Mercier Archive)**

*Left:*
Elizabeth MacCurtain, Tomás MacCurtain's wife, was continually harassed by the Black and Tans and Auxiliaries after the death of her husband. Her home was frequently raided and on occasion shots were fired in her direction. (Courtesy of Fionnuala Mac Curtain)

*Below:*
MacCurtain's funeral was attended by prominent Republicans from all over the country as well as the men of his brigade. A massive show of strength by the Republicans, this must have been a major concern to the British forces in Cork. (Courtesy of Mercier Archive)

The circumstances of the murder were the subject of a historic inquest, conducted by Coroner James. J. McCabe, in which ninety-seven witnesses were examined, sixty-four of whom were police, thirty-one civilians and two military. The inquest was opened on the day of the shooting itself and concluded on 17 April 1920 with the following unanimous verdict:

> We find the late Alderman MacCurtain, Lord Mayor of Cork, died from shock and haemorrhage caused by bullet wounds, and that he was wilfully murdered under circumstances of the most callous brutality, and that the murder was organised and carried out by the Royal Irish Constabulary, officially directed by the British Government, and we return a verdict of wilful murder against David Lloyd George, Prime Minister of England; Lord French, Lord Lieutenant of Ireland; Ian McPherson, late Chief Secretary of Ireland; Acting Inspector General Smith of the Royal Irish Constabulary; Divisional Inspector Clayton of the Royal Irish Constabulary; District Inspector Swanzy and some unknown members of the Royal Irish Constabulary. We strongly condemn the system at present in vogue of carrying out raids at unreasonable hours. We tender to Mrs MacCurtain and family our sincerest sympathy. We extend to the citizens of Cork our sympathy in the loss that they have sustained by the death of one so eminently capable of directing their civic administration.

At the inquest RIC County Inspector Maloney revealed that on 19 March he had received orders from the military authorities to arrest MacCurtain. This was to be a combined military and RIC operation. As a result he sent the order to District Inspector Swanzy, whose division MacCurtain lived in. Swanzy said in his evidence to the inquest: 'I was not ordered to arrest the Lord Mayor, but I was ordered to detail police to indicate the house of the Lord Mayor to a military party.' Lieutenant F. Cooke stated that on 19 March he was detailed to take charge of a party of twenty men to report to King Street RIC Barracks at 2 a.m. the following morning to carry out the arrest. He was joined there by a sergeant and three constables and was informed then, for the first time, who was to be arrested – Tomás MacCurtain. But when he arrived at the lord mayor's house, he was informed that MacCurtain had been shot dead earlier that morning. Considering it his duty to search the

The funeral procession moves along Camden Quay. MacCurtain was laid to rest in the Republican Plot in St Finbarr's Cemetery. (Courtesy of Mercier Archive)

house, he did so, including the bed on which the remains of the lord mayor were lying. Major General Strickland later confirmed that the authority for the arrest came from the commander-in-chief in Ireland.

Why such an early morning raid was planned is unclear. The police were well aware that the lord mayor could be found at his office in City Hall during the day while attending to the duties of his office. They could also have found him at the public functions he carried out. It would have been entirely unnecessary for an armed force to raid his house early in the morning simply to arrest him.

It was generally believed in Cork that the murder of MacCurtain was premeditated by members of the RIC and was a reprisal for the shooting of Constable

*Above left:*
**An RIC man standing outside the police barracks door at King Street (MacCurtain Street), where many of those involved in the murder of Tomás MacCurtain were stationed. (Author's collection)**

*Above right:*
**The RIC barracks at King Street was destroyed by the IRA in July 1920 in retaliation for the killing of Tomás MacCurtain. (Courtesy of the *Irish Examiner*)**

Murtagh at Pope's Quay, assuming that such an action could have been planned and carried out within the short time frame that separated the attack on the house and the military raid just after 2 a.m. Murtagh had been attached to the Sundays Well Barracks and eyewitness accounts prove that a large force far in excess of the number of RIC men stationed in the nearby King Street Barracks was involved. A direct link to those responsible was provided by the discovery of a button from an RIC tunic at the door of the MacCurtain house by local postman Mick Goggin following the murder.

In the wake of MacCurtain's assassination there was an increase in IRA activity.

The Cork IRA was out to avenge MacCurtain by identifying and killing those involved in his murder, and a number of RIC men were shot in the months following as a direct result. The most prominent of these was Detective Inspector Oswald Ross Swanzy, the officer accused of ordering the killing, who was shot and killed in Lisburn on Sunday 22 August 1920 with MacCurtain's gun. The violence would continue to escalate throughout the year, and with the arrival of the Black and Tans and the Auxiliaries, things would only get worse.

## THE DEATH OF TERENCE MacSWINEY

MacCurtain's successor as both lord mayor and commanding officer of Cork No. 1 Brigade was Terence MacSwiney. MacSwiney was born in Cork city on 28 March 1879 to a well-respected family and his father was a tobacco manufacturer. Like MacCurtain, the young MacSwiney attended the North Monastery school, where he excelled in Irish and Irish history. At the age of fifteen, after the failure of his father's tobacco business, Terence went to work at Dwyer & Co. in Washington Street and was employed for seventeen years with this firm, where he rose to the position of accountant in 1911. He then left Dwyer's and became a commercial teacher for the Municipal School of Commerce. He was soon involved in writing articles for various national newspapers and reduced the number of hours he slept to allow him to write and study. His first book, *Music of Freedom*, a lengthy poem promoting his desire for Ireland's freedom, was published in 1905.

In December 1913, together with Tomás MacCurtain, Seán O'Hegarty and J. J. Walsh, MacSwiney formed the first Cork branch of the Volunteers. While his great friend MacCurtain was a brilliant military organiser, MacSwiney's talent lay in public speaking and writing. He published his own newspaper, *Fianna Fáil*, which he used as a platform to promote Irish nationalism. The British authorities suppressed this republican organ after just eleven issues.

When MacCurtain was murdered, MacSwiney did not shirk from his responsibilities and was unanimously elected to replace MacCurtain as lord mayor. In his position as the second republican lord mayor of Cork he had to take precautions,

· 1920 ·

ALDERMAN MacSWINEY,
Lord Mayor of Cork.

A republican card showing Terence MacSwiney. (Author's collection)

as the British authorities were determined to be rid of this man who had become a thorn in their side. Concealed doors were installed in the City Hall so that he could get away in the event of a British raid. However, these failed to prevent the inevitable. On 12 August 1920 City Hall was raided by a considerable British Army contingent of six armoured cars and six lorries full of soldiers. The lord mayor was arrested and charged with illegally possessing a cipher key to decode military dispatches. He was ordered to hand over his chain of office, which he refused to do; it was then forcibly removed but was returned to him the following day. When asked if he wished to have legal representation, according to Moirin Chevasse in her biography of MacSwiney, he replied: 'The position is that I am Lord Mayor of Cork and Chief Magistrate of this city. I declare that this court is illegal and those that take part in it are liable to arrest under the laws of the Republic …'

MacSwiney was sentenced to two years' imprisonment but, having gone on hunger strike on the day he was arrested, he stated that 'I will be free within a month either alive or dead.' On the previous day, 11 August, a mass hunger strike had been initiated in Cork Gaol by incarcerated IRA members, most of whom were being held without charge or trial. Those prisoners were demanding that either they be given the status of political prisoners or, if not, that they be released.

MacSwiney was put on board a British naval vessel in the early hours of the morning of 17 August and transported to Brixton Prison for his incarceration. There, the prison doctor judged him to be in such a poor state that he would not survive force-feeding. The British authorities tried to keep him alive; their aim was to defeat him, not to make him a martyr. However, as the hunger strike went on it became headline news around the world. Journalists from all corners of the globe descended on Brixton, much to the embarrassment of the British authorities. This Irishman was taking on the might of the British Empire by offering himself as a sacrifice for a cause he was prepared to die for. King George V was actually prepared to pardon him, and British trade unions supported his release, but despite prayers, protests, appeals and even work stoppages, both at home and abroad, the British government refused any sort of compromise.

As each day passed, the lord mayor became weaker and weaker until, on the seventy-fifth day of his hunger strike, Terence MacSwiney died. Soon after his death, Michael Collins and Arthur Griffith ordered any remaining hunger strikers off their hunger strikes. But it was too late to save Michael Fitzgerald, who died the week before MacSwiney, after sixty-seven days on hunger strike, and Joseph Murphy, aged twenty-two, who died after seventy-six days without food, two hours before MacSwiney. The remaining prisoners on hunger strike ended their fast on 12 November 1920, as ordered.

The British authorities prevented republicans parading MacSwiney's body through the streets of Dublin, mindful of the reaction following the execution of the leaders after the Easter Rising. The body was instead sent directly to Queenstown (Cobh) on board the *Rathmore* and eventually transferred to the admiralty tug the *Mary Tavy*, which carried it to the city. Tens of thousands of people filed past his body whilst it lay in state in City Hall. MacSwiney's requiem mass was celebrated by the bishop of Cork, assisted by four Irish bishops and two Australian bishops. On 1 November 1920 he was buried in the Republican Plot at St Finbarr's Cemetery, alongside his friend and predecessor Tomás MacCurtain.

**The tricolour-draped coffin of MacSwiney is carried through the streets of Cork. His Volunteer Cronje hat rests on top of the tricolour. (Courtesy of Mercier Archive)**

*Above:*
MacSwiney lying in state in City Hall. The building was frequently targeted for attack because it was seen as a Republican stronghold. (Courtesy of Mercier Archive)

*Left:*
Queues formed outside City Hall of those waiting to pay their respects to the body of MacSwiney. (Courtesy of the *Irish Examiner*)

*Above:*

The solemn removal of the coffin of MacSwiney from City Hall, before it begins its procession through the streets of Cork. (Courtesy of the *Irish Examiner*)

*Below:*

As with MacCurtain's funeral, massive crowds lined the streets to pay their respects to MacSwiney. In this photograph the cortege proceeds along Patrick Street, with large floral bouquets carried in front of the coffin. (Author's collection)

# DONAL O'CALLAGHAN,

## THIRD REPUBLICAN LORD MAYOR OF CORK

When Terence MacSwiney was elected to the position of lord mayor, Donal O'Callaghan became his deputy lord mayor. Following the death of MacSwiney, O'Callaghan was elected to succeed the late lord mayor by Cork Corporation on 4 November 1920. He was the third successive republican mayor to be elected in Cork and he now became a target for the British forces, like his predecessors before him. Before it was burned down, City Hall was constantly watched and raided, and many council meetings were cancelled due to impending raids. O'Callaghan spent his time constantly moving from house to house at night, on the run, carefully keeping his eyes and ears open for unwelcome visitors.

In February 1921 Donal O'Callaghan and Peter MacSwiney, brother of the deceased lord mayor, were invited to give evidence to the American Commission on Conditions in Ireland, established to record an impartial account of the atrocities committed in Ireland by both sides during the War of Independence, including the burning of Cork. As the British authorities were prepared to do everything in their power to prevent the two men giving evidence, the only way they could travel was to stow away on a ship. Many witnesses had been intimidated and shot at to dissuade them from testifying to the commission. Whilst on board ship O'Callaghan became violently seasick and they were both discovered, so the captain made them work their passage as seamen.

When they first arrived in America, the State Department tried to deport them because they had entered the country illegally as stowaways. O'Callaghan, as lord mayor of Cork, claimed special status as a political refugee, and pressure from Irish-American trade union representatives led the Department of Labour to intervene and insist that, because they had worked their passage, they were in the country legally. As a result, both men were granted leave to remain in the USA. O'Callaghan and MacSwiney testified as witnesses before the commission, which had been organised by Oswald Garrison Villard, editor of *The Nation*, a New York liberal weekly. Their evidence was published in *Evidence on Conditions in Ireland*,

Donal O'Callaghan, the third republican lord mayor of Cork, whose life was under constant threat from the Black and Tans. (Courtesy of Cork Public Museum)

transcribed and annotated by Albert Coyle, official reporter to the commission. In his evidence, O'Callaghan described a litany of abuses by the crown forces in Cork in the months before the burning of Cork, including the beating of priests, attacks

on women and 'wanton murder', as well as a catalogue of arson attacks in the city. When asked whom he felt was responsible for the destruction of 11 December, he clearly stated, 'I charge definitely the British Crown forces in Cork.'

**In this image most of the windows in City Hall have been smashed by members of the crown forces sometime before the main burning. A corporation worker is checking that the hoarding is stoutly in place. (Courtesy of Mercier Archive)**

The American Shoe Co. at No. 45 Patrick Street was one of the November victims of arson in Cork city. (Courtesy of the *Irish Examiner*)

# ARSON RAMPANT IN CORK

On 17 July 1920 Lieutenant Colonel Gerald Brice Ferguson Smyth, the divisional police commissioner and one of those mentioned at the subsequent inquest as being responsible for the death of Tomás MacCurtain, was shot dead inside the County Club on the South Mall in Cork city by the IRA. Combined with increased IRA activity across the county, this led Major General Peter Strickland, commander of the 6th Infantry Division, whose designated area of operations was Munster, to issue the following curfew order, printed in *The Cork Examiner* on 20 July 1920:

I do hereby order and require every person within the area specified in the schedule hereto to remain within doors between the hours of 10 o'clock p.m. and 3 o'clock a.m., unless provided with a permit in writing from the competent military authority or some person duly authorised by him.

Schedule – All the area within a radius of three miles of the General Post Office, Pembroke Street, in the city of Cork.

Permits will be granted to clergymen, registered medical practitioners, and nurses engaged on urgent duties. Permits will not be granted to other persons save in the case of absolute necessity.

Every person abroad between the hours mentioned in the foregoing order, when challenged by any policeman, or by an officer, NCO, or soldier on duty, must immediately halt and obey the orders given to him, and if he fails to do so, it will be at his own peril.

This order left the streets of the city largely deserted between 10 p.m. and 3 a.m. every night, except for members of the British forces on patrol. The months that

Hoardings had been placed in the windows of City Hall in an attempt to prevent incendiaries being thrown through them. The broken glass in this picture is evidence of earlier attacks. (Courtesy of Mercier Archive)

followed would see numerous fires in Cork city started deliberately during curfew hours when there was no one around to witness who was involved.

On 21 November 1920, at 1.25 a.m., Messrs Dwyer & Co., Washington Street, one of the largest wholesale warehouses in Cork, was broken into. A very determined effort was made to burn the premises, but fortunately it failed as the sprinkler system activated and saved the warehouse. Not only were petrol canisters found on the premises, but bales of wool and cotton were found stretched along the corridors, and the stairs were saturated with petrol. An insurance claim was agreed with the assessors for the sum of £2,592.

As a result of the abduction of Tom Dowling, a British serviceman, and the shooting of County Inspector Robert Madden in Cork city, on 24 November the building on Hardwick Street housing the Brian Boru Piper's Club and Sinn Féin Club was burned. The next day No. 56 Grand Parade, which housed the Artane Clothing Co. and the Sinn Féin headquarters, suffered the same fate.

Between Saturday 27 November and Sunday 28 November, fires were started at a number of premises. By 4 a.m. on Saturday morning the fire brigade had been called to Forrest's premises in 33–34 Patrick Street, which was well ablaze. On the same morning two houses on North Main Street, a house in St Augustine Street, the recreation hall in Douglas, and St Michael's GAA Club in Blackrock were also destroyed. By 1.50 a.m. on 28 November three adjoining premises – the American Shoe Co. at No. 45, Blackthorn House, at No. 46 and Cahill & Co. at No. 47 Patrick Street, on the corner with Princes Street – were alight. While the latter two premises were incinerated, the American Shoe Co. survived until 1 December when it was once again set on fire and this time destroyed. Also on 28 November, the jewellery shop of Michael Roche was broken into during curfew hours, and goods valued at several thousand pounds, including sixty-two watches, gold chains and gold and silver jewellery, were stolen.

In the early hours of 29 November the ITGWU headquarters at No. 8 Camden Quay was set alight by British forces. At 2 a.m. the fire brigade was called and the fire extinguished, but the building was set fire to again later that morning. The fire brigade was again called and attempted to reach the fire, but the men were shot at and prevented from extinguishing the second fire, ensuring that the headquarters and its neighbouring buildings were gutted. Later that day, Cork No. 1 Brigade abducted father and son Frederick and James Blemens, who they suspected of being informers.

The following day, an attempt was made to set City Hall on fire, while Egan's, which had been looted only days previously, was set alight. Despite being threatened at gunpoint, the city's firemen managed to extinguish this blaze. That day also saw the destruction of the Thomas Ashe Sinn Féin Club on Fr Mathew Quay.

On 1 December, at 4 a.m., Dalton's restaurant on King Street (now MacCurtain Street) was burned and O'Gorman's drapery shop on the same street was looted before it was set alight and destroyed. Hats, overcoats, raincoats, suits, pyjamas, silk handkerchiefs and other stock were taken. The Royal Liver Assurance Society in Victoria Buildings on King Street and Barriscalle's jewellers shop on Bridge Street were also looted. Gold and silver watches and a large quantity of rings, brooches and other jewellery were taken from the latter.

*Right:*

The premises of the ITGWU on Camden Quay after its destruction. (Author's collection)

*Below left:*

The sampling of stolen goods from a Cork store by crown forces was normal! (Courtesy of Mercier Archive)

*Below right:*

Michael Roche's jewellery shop was looted on 28 November. The looting of jewellery shops proved to be a lucrative occupation for Auxiliaries and Black and Tans. (Author's collection)

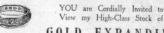

—USEFUL—
## Christmas Presents

YOU are Cordially Invited to View my High-Class Stock of

### GOLD EXPANDING WRISTLET WATCHES.

Bracelets, Brooches, Dress Rings, Pendants, Signet Rings. Gold Alberts, Tie Pins, Links, etc., Manicure Sets, Toilet Sets.

Silver Chain Bags, Silver Purses, plain, engraved, and engine turned.

Cigarette Cases, Card Cases, etc., etc.,

LARGE SELECTION TO CHOOSE FROM ALL THE NEWEST DESIGNS.

## M. ROCHE,

Watchmaker, Jeweller,
and
Diamond Merchant.

### 61, PATRICK ST. CORK.

A man poses for the camera as a Shawlie passes him outside the burned-out premises of Forrest & Sons, which was gutted on 27 November. (Courtesy of the *Irish Examiner*)

A soldier lights up a cigarette as an armoured car passes the old City Hall. The blackened windows and timber hoarding show the signs of one of the attempted arson attacks on the building in 1920. (Courtesy of Cork Public Museum)

Donal O'Callaghan's report to the American Commission, taken from newspaper reports collected over the month of December 1920, conveyed the atmosphere in which people lived, despite these outrages. A preliminary newspaper report, from around 6 December, dealt with outrages committed by various sections of crown forces in Cork city and county in November 1920. It detailed:

280 arrests; upwards of 50 attempted arrests; 4 publicly placarded threats to the citizens of Cork; hundreds of general outrages; 15 trains held up; upwards of 200 curfew arrests, of which 74 were made the night William Mulcahy was shot [at Bachelor's Quay near

the North Gate Bridge for failing to stop when ordered by the military], the majority of which were made before 10 p.m. when curfew begins; four Sinn Féin Cumanns (clubs) burned to the ground; 12 large business houses burned to the ground; many attempts made to fire others, including the City Hall on two occasions; amount of damage done by fire estimated at £1,000,000; seven men were shot dead; upwards of 12 men dangerously wounded by shots; attempted assassination of upwards of 10; upwards of 500 houses of private citizens forcibly entered and searched; much indiscriminate shooting.

The report finishes by stating that 'the majority of these outrages were committed during curfew hours, namely, from 10 p.m. to 3 a.m.', which meant they must have been carried out by British forces.

In such an atmosphere of turmoil it would have been difficult to carry on day-to-day business. From Tuesday 3 June 1919 to 11 December 1920 Roches Stores operated during the general turmoil that existed in Cork. Augustine Walsh, secretary of the store, recalled: 'On one occasion a bomb was thrown in the street, just outside our premises, and metal fragments of the bomb came hurtling through the door into the warehouse, but fortunately no one was injured.' The constant worry of carrying on business in the midst of troubled conditions had to be taken as a matter of course. However, the curfews, raids, shootings, ambushes, bomb-throwing, searches, etc., which became the usual routine were not conducive to the orderly building-up of a business. William Roche's worries would only have been added to when 'Reports then began to circulate that one side of the conflicting forces had grown impatient with the methods of petty warfare adopted by their opponents and intended teaching them a lesson by burning down the principal business warehouses in Patrick Street, including Roches Stores.'

The building which faced the greatest threat in the city was City Hall. As mentioned above, with a series of Republican lord mayors being elected, it came to be regarded by the British forces as a hotbed of Republicanism and, unsurprisingly, became a particular target of British ire. The old City Hall contained the largest concert hall in Cork with seating capacity for 2,000. This hall had one of the finest organs in Ireland at the time, which was created by William Magahey for the Cork Exhibition of 1902–3 and was subsequently installed in the concert venue. City Hall was also the main municipal building in the city and the offices of the lord mayor, town clerk, the city engineers, city solicitors and the public health department were all located within it. The council chambers, lord mayor's rooms, committee rooms and the rooms for the members of Cork Corporation were all at the front of the building. One of the most unfortunate results of the burning of City Hall was that all the city records up to that time were destroyed.

City Hall was attacked on a number of occasions before it was finally destroyed. At approximately 9 p.m. on Sunday 18 July 1920, Patrick O'Connell, the lamp lighter, was on his way to the lighting department in City Hall when he heard shots being fired on Parnell Street. On his arrival at City Hall, he discovered that two strangers had taken shelter there, one of whom was a woman. O'Connell was in the watchman's quarters when, not long afterwards, a number of policemen appeared outside one of the side doors. The men were ordered to open the door immediately and the watchman did so. O'Connell's account, quoted in the American Commission's report, continues: 'They lined us up against the wall and kept us in that position for 20 minutes with our hands over our heads all the time. The woman continually beseeched them … to have mercy on us …They replied, "What mercy had ye on us?" … They all had strange English accents.' As the intruders were leaving, 'we could then hear them smashing the windows of the City Hall. They all seemed to be under the influence of drink.'

Because of frequent attempts to burn City Hall following this incident, from the start of October a fireman was always on duty at City Hall and lines of hose were kept in readiness. One such attempt is recorded in detail in the American Commission's report. At 4.05 a.m. on Saturday 9 October, Captain Hutson received a call at Sullivan's Quay fire station saying that City Hall was on fire. Upon the fire brigade's arrival, they found the waterworks' office at the front of the building ablaze. According to Hutson, the glass of the windows had 'burned out' and the lath work within the room was in danger of catching fire. Luckily the fire was brought under control in about half an hour. Captain Hutson observed that the rapid spread of the conflagration could only have been due to the use of an accelerant like petrol, paraffin or benzene. He found a piece of a bomb on the pavement on the Albert Quay side and it became apparent that the fire had been started by bombs thrown over the hoardings protecting the windows after 'some inflammable material must

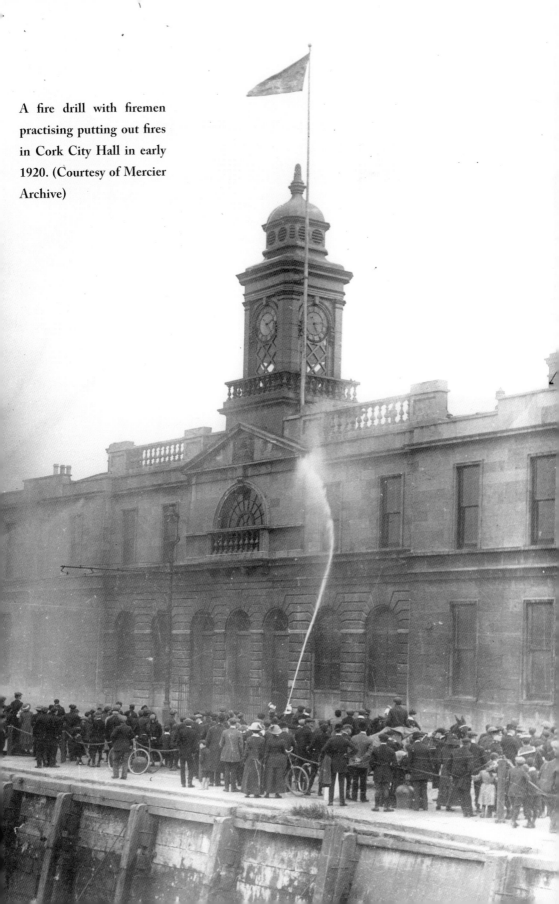

A fire drill with firemen practising putting out fires in Cork City Hall in early 1920. (Courtesy of Mercier Archive)

have been poured into the waterworks office'. When the room itself was examined it was clear that one of the doors had been knocked off its hinges by the force of the explosions and had fallen into the room. Hutson remarked that it was only the 'powerful' dividing wall of the public office which prevented the flames from spreading to this adjoining room, but an attempt had been made to burn it too, as a bomb was found lodged in a desk and splinters marked the walls.

Following the departure of the fire brigade, the night watchman, Timothy Ring, closed all the doors and stayed on duty until 7 a.m. He later overheard some RIC men say, 'Well it has been a failure again this time, but the next time we will finish it.' Later events would prove him correct.

**Cork under siege in June 1920 – sandbags, barbed wire and Lewis guns became typical scenes of the British controlling the city by force. Here the men are stationed outside the courthouse. (Author's collection)**

*Left:*
Tanks patrol the area or Summerhill near St Luke's church in 1920. (Courtesy of Brid Hughes)

*Below:*

Soldiers cordon off a crowd outside a Beamish & Crawford pub (now Gallagher's pub, MacCurtain Street). (Courtesy of the *Irish Examiner*)

General Tom Barry, who led the successful ambush at Kilmichael in November 1920. (Courtesy of Mercier Archive)

# THE KILMICHAEL AMBUSH

On 28 November 1920 a flying column of IRA men led by Tom Barry took up position at its chosen ambush site on a section of the Macroom to Dunmanway road between Kilmichael and Gleann. The events that took place there later that day would have widespread repercussions across Ireland, but nowhere more so than in Cork city.

The target of the ambush was the Auxiliaries, who had killed a civilian, James Lehane, at Ballymakeera on 17 October 1920, and in November carried out a number of raids on the villages in the area surrounding Macroom, where they were based – Dunmanway, Coppeen and Castletownkenneigh. In his memoir, *Guerilla Days in Ireland*, Tom Barry noted that the IRA had hardly fired a shot at the Auxiliaries, which 'had a very serious effect on the morale of the whole people as well as on the IRA'. His assessment was that the West Cork IRA needed a successful action against the Auxiliaries to counteract this situation and so, along with Volunteer Michael McCarthy, Barry scouted possible ambush sites on horseback and selected a place on the road that the Auxiliaries coming out of Macroom used every day.

On 21 November Barry assembled a flying column of thirty-six riflemen at Clogher. After a week's training, the column marched to the ambush site on foot through the night and took up positions in the low rocky hills on either side of the road on the morning of 28 November. They had thirty-five rounds for each rifle as well as a handful of revolvers and two Mills bombs. It was a risky operation as, unlike most IRA ambush positions, there was no obvious escape route for the guerrillas should the fighting go against them.

As the Auxiliaries, in two lorries, came into view that afternoon, five armed IRA men, who had arrived unannounced just as the enemy had been sighted, nearly upset Barry's plans, but they were quickly diverted up a side road. The Auxiliaries' first lorry slowed down because Barry placed himself on the road wearing an IRA officer's tunic. The British later claimed Barry was wearing a British uniform and indeed, Barry had relied on this assumption to ensure that his adversaries in the lorries would not simply drive on. The British later alleged that over 100 IRA fighters were present wearing British uniforms and steel trench helmets. Barry, however, insisted that, apart from him, the ambush party was in civilian attire, though they used captured British weapons and equipment.

The first lorry, containing nine Auxiliaries, slowed almost to a halt close to the intended ambush position, where, on the north side of the road, Sections One (ten riflemen) and Two (ten riflemen) lay concealed. At this point Barry threw a Mills bomb into the cab of the first lorry that exploded, killing the driver. As the first lorry rolled to a stop, a savage close-quarter fight ensued between the Auxiliaries in the back and the IRA in Section One along with Barry and his three-person command-post group, who had been stationed close by. According to Barry's account, some of the British were killed using rifle butts and bayonets in what was a brutal and bloody encounter. This part of the battle was over relatively quickly, with all nine Auxiliaries left dead or dying. The British later claimed that the dead from both lorries had been mutilated with axes, although Barry dismissed this as atrocity propaganda.

While this fight was going on, the second lorry, also containing nine Auxiliaries had stopped near Section Two of the IRA. Its occupants were in a more advantageous position than those of the first lorry because they were further away from their ambushing group. They quickly dismounted from the lorry onto the road, where they exchanged fire with the IRA, killing Michael McCarthy. Barry and the three men from the command post now moved to attack these Auxiliaries from the rear. Barry claimed their opponents called out 'We surrender' and that some dropped their rifles, but when three IRA men emerged from cover they opened fire again with revolvers. Jim O'Sullivan was killed instantly, while Pat Deasy was mortally wounded. Barry records in *Guerilla Days* that he then ordered, 'Rapid fire and do not stop until I tell you!' He ignored a subsequent attempt by the remaining Auxiliaries to surrender, and his men kept firing, advancing to within a range of ten yards, until they believed all the Auxiliaries were dead. Meda Ryan records that Barry later said of the Auxiliaries who tried to surrender a second time, 'soldiers who had cheated in war deserved to die'. He referred to the Auxiliaries' first surrender as a 'false surrender'.

At the conclusion of the fight, the IRA believed they had killed all of the Auxiliaries, but two had survived. One, Lieutenant H. F. Forde, was unconscious after receiving a head wound but survived the injury. The other, Cadet Cecil Guthrie, who initially escaped from the ambush, was captured later that day by the IRA and shot dead. Among the sixteen British dead on the road at Kilmichael was Francis Crake, commander of the Auxiliaries in Macroom. The inquest into the killings recorded that he was killed by a gunshot wound.

The political fallout from the Kilmichael ambush outweighed its military significance. While the British forces in Ireland, over 30,000 strong, could easily absorb eighteen casualties, the fact that the IRA had been able to wipe out a whole patrol of elite Auxiliaries was, for them, deeply shocking. The British forces in the West Cork area took immediate revenge on the local population by burning several houses, shops and barns in Kilmichael, Johnstown and Inchigeela, including all of the houses around the ambush site. The ambush would also have severe ramifications for Cork city. Over the next few nights several premises in the city centre were set on fire and there can be little doubt that what happened at Kilmichael, combined with later events, spurred on the forces that destroyed large swathes of Cork just two weeks later.

The remains of Brian Dillon's house. (Author's collection)

# THE DILLON'S CROSS AMBUSH

According to a *Cork Examiner* report of 18 December:

> The residents of St Luke's and the immediate neighbourhood have been envied very frequently on their immunity from participation in the serious disturbances which have taken place in other parts of the city, but they are no longer as safe as they have been heretofore. This is the direct result of the dreadful occurrence which took place there on Saturday night, and which has resulted in not alone the destruction of many houses in the locality, but also the wiping out of a very substantial portion of the principal business centre of Cork. Somewhere between 7.30 and 7.40 on Saturday evening the inhabitants of the district were greatly startled by, first an exceedingly loud explosion and then two or three others in rapid succession not quite so loud.

The loud explosions heard by the residents of Dillon's Cross were the result of an attack by an IRA ambush party on a patrol of Auxiliaries from K Company on the evening of 11 December, during which grenades were lobbed into one of the Crossley tenders carrying the patrol. The *Examiner*'s report continued:

> For a considerable time none except those who were parties to the outrage and the unfortunate occupants of the lorry who were the victims realised what happened. But when the dense clouds caused by the smoke and falling splinters had disappeared it was discovered that at least a dozen were wounded, one of whom subsequently died. The auxiliary policemen were coming from the direction of the military barracks at the time. This the [*sic*] ambush was apparently done from a dead wall on the Old Youghal Road, where the thoroughfare runs into Dillon's Cross when travelling from the direction of

the barracks; as there is practically a right-hand angle turn here, over a very short stretch of road, all cars must of necessity pull up to a dead slow pace. This fact, together with the existence of the dead wall, lent itself to the purpose of an ambush, and the deadly effect with which it was carried out is already mentioned.

The site of the ambush was just 100 metres from Victoria Barracks, where the Auxiliaries were based. Auxiliary Spencer Chapman was mortally wounded and died the following day.

With the benefit of hindsight, the *Examiner* was not impressed by this IRA attack, for largely practical reasons:

It is difficult however to understand the mentality of the individual who conceived such an attack, for, surely, whatever his ideas of warfare might be the inhabitants of this densely populated district were entitled to some consideration, and indeed it is most probable that very few or any of them had the remotest notion of what was about to take place. Certain it is, however, that in the space of a few short seconds at least a dozen men were nearly hurtled into eternity without a moment's warning and one of them has since gone to his maker. The uninjured members of the party speedily attended to their wounded comrades and quickly moved them to Mr O'Hare's victualling establishment known as Brian Dillon's house, where they remained until an ambulance had been summoned from the barracks and the unfortunate men taken to hospital.

What happened next gave a foretaste of the events that would occur in the city centre later that evening. Lorry-loads of Auxiliaries and British soldiers arrived on the scene and began to exact revenge for the ambush and the wounding of their comrades. The *Examiner* describes what happened next:

Some time after 8 o'clock a series of burnings began at Dillon's Cross and those were practically continuous until day dawned. Under such circumstances, it was not surprising that those living in the neighbourhood spent a terrifying night and many fervent prayers were offered that the dawn of day would not bring further turmoil. Prior to the burnings

*Right:*

**An army tank is used to demolish the gable wall of Brian Dillon's house after it was burned out by British forces. (Courtesy of Cork Public Museum)**

a civilian had been wounded, but his condition or the nature of his wounds were not of a serious nature. A small row of houses run from the vicinity of this shop on the northern side of the Old Youghal Road and the extreme one of those was then set on fire and as there was no assistance available it was burned to the ground, while the occupant of the adjoining house was compelled to remove his furniture on to the street. The furniture was then saturated with petrol or some such substance and set on fire, the house however being left untouched.

Brian Dillon's house … was next visited and though the four walls are still standing, the remainder of the building has been completely gutted. Next the house No. 10, Bridget Villas was attended to, but there was no person in residence at the time, and some of the furniture had been removed some weeks ago. Another house on the opposite side and a little lower down was also attacked, this shortly after the lorries containing the curfew patrol had passed down. The only occupants of the house a lady and her young brother, who were given a peremptory order to clear out and were refused time to even get their hats, let alone a considerable sum of money in notes which were in the upstairs portion of the house. They made their way as quickly as they could to the house of a friend and the lady who was in rather a weak state of health nearly collapsed when she was admitted. Even then, the residents of the locality had not fully recognised the night of terror that was before them.

At various times during the night rifle shots rang out and in the stillness, a stillness broken only by the crackling of the burning timber of the houses on fire, those shots had a most terrifying effect, for no one knew seeing that houses were being burned when his turn would come next. Coming on towards morning, loud knocking on their doors startled the residents of Harrington's Row and a couple of them were opened. The occupants were questioned on their political leanings, and one of them, an ex-soldier and his wife, were compelled to sing 'God Save the King' the lady being coached in the words by her husband.

Practically no damage was done in this house, but the one next door was almost completely burned. The man who resides here was ordered out of doors at the point of a revolver. He was in his stocking vamps, however, and while his captors went back into the house for a moment, he ran for his life, and succeeded in getting away. He returned when daylight dawned, to find his effects practically gone but was greatly relieved to find that nothing had happened to his wife. Further down the road the occupant of a house was ordered out, and placed with his back against a wall, where he was told he would be shot, but the threat was not carried out.

Similar scenes of terror and devastation were soon repeated throughout Cork's city centre.

## THE SHOOTING OF THE DELANY BROTHERS

The fires were not the only violent consequence of the events at Dillon's Cross. Following the ambush Seán O'Donoghue, who had commanded the IRA's ambush party, and Volunteer James O'Mahony, who had taken part, made their way towards the Delany farmhouse at Dublin Hill in the north of the city. The Republican Delany family were well known to the authorities and Jeremiah and Cornelius Delany were volunteers in the 1st Battalion of Cork No. 1 Brigade. O'Donoghue hid a number of unused grenades on the farm before he and O'Mahony went their separate ways.

It is thought that, while searching the site of the ambush, the Auxiliaries found a cap belonging to one of these two men and used bloodhounds to follow the scent, which led them to the Delany home. Retribution for the ambush was to be swift and savage. Daniel Delany gave this account for the Irish Labour Party's report on the burning of Cork:

About 2 a.m. a number of men came to my door and demanded admission in a loud voice, and beat the door harshly. I opened the door, and they called me out. The man who seemed to be in command asked if I was a Sinn Feiner. I answered, 'I don't understand you.' He then said, 'Are you interested in politics?' I answered, 'I am an old man and not interested in anything.' He then asked, 'Who is inside?' I said 'Nobody but my family.' 'Can I see them?' said he. 'Certainly,' I said. 'They are in bed.' He asked me to show them up.

At least eight men entered the house and went upstairs. A large crowd remained outside, as I could hear them moving and see them in the yard. The men who went upstairs entered my sons' bedroom and said, in a harsh voice, 'Get up out of that.' I was in the room with them. My sons got up and stood at the bedside. They asked them if their name was Delany. My sons answered, 'Yes.' At that moment I heard distinctly two or more shots, and my two boys fell immediately.

Immediately after, my brother-in-law, William Dunlea, who was sleeping in the same room in another bed, was fired on by the same party and wounded in two places. My brother-in-law is over sixty years of age. As far as I could see, they wore long overcoats, and spoke with a strong English accent.

When one of their sisters entered the boys' bedroom, she observed Jeremiah lying on the floor. His lips were still moving, but he died shortly afterwards. Con was lying in a pool of blood in the bed, but was still clinging to life. A phone call was made from the nearest telephone office and an ambulance was requested from the fire station, but none was available due to the fires that were now raging through the city. It took until about 4 a.m. before a priest from the North Cathedral arrived. An ambulance was again requested at 8 a.m. and finally arrived. It brought Cornelius to the Mercy Hospital, where he finally succumbed to his wounds on 18 December.

*Left:*
The only surviving photograph of Jeremiah Delany, murdered at his home by crown forces following the Dillon's Cross ambush. (Courtesy of Mercier Archive)

*Below:*
Bloodhounds were often used to track IRA suspects. Unfortunately for the Delany brothers these hounds led a party of Auxiliaries to their home, where they were brutally murdered. (Courtesy of Mercier Archive)

*Left*:
The only surviving photograph of Cornelius Delany, brother of Jeremiah, who died a week later at the Mercy Hospital. (Courtesy of Cork Public Museum)

The funeral of Cornelius Delany of Dublin Hill, who was brutally murdered by British forces, passing the ruins of a devastated Patrick Street. (Courtesy of the *Irish Examiner*)

# THE BURNING OF THE CITY

While the Dillon's Cross ambush was not the sole reason for the destruction of the commercial heart of the city – premeditated plans were in place to carry out this task well in advance of the ambush – it served to expedite the devastation which was to befall Cork city. Around 9 p.m. that evening, before the official curfew began at 10 p.m., the British military started to fire indiscriminately at civilians, in order to clear all the principal streets in the city. According to *Irish Weekly Independent* of 18 December:

> … the Rev. P. McSweeney, chaplain to the Good Shepherds and professor in Farren-ferris, while returning home at about 9 o'clock on 11 December is alleged to have been taken out of the tram at St Luke's corner and assaulted by five or six armed men who boarded and stopped the tram. It was witnessed that they tore off Fr McSweeney's over-coat, vest and collar and kicked his breviary. The other passengers, including four women and eight men, were ordered off the tram. The men were made to stand against a wall. One of the armed men, pointing to Fr McSweeney, said, 'We have a Papist bastard at last.' The men were ordered to go and then Fr McSweeney was ordered to write, 'to hell with the Pope'. He said surely you could not ask a Catholic Priest to do that. He was again assaulted and told 'clear' and his clothes were kicked towards him. He gathered up his clothes and ran to his residence which was a few hundred yards nearby. On the

*Opposite:*
**Hilser Brothers, Grand Parade, became a high-class target due to its expensive jewellery and gold collection which could be easily disposed of and sold. (Author's collection)**

same night at 9.15 p.m. the Rev. F. McCarthy, chaplain to the Incurable Hospital, was walking from St Patrick's church towards his residence in St Luke's and armed men at Summerhill stopped him. He was assaulted and prodded with a bayonet and told to run. Whilst he was running, five shots were fired, fortunately none met their target. He managed to get home safely.

At 10.30 p.m. the first official call to the Cork City Fire Brigade was received, reporting that the department store of Grant & Co. on Patrick Street was on fire. Because of the speedy response of the fire brigade, this premises was initially saved, but worse was to follow. Both The Munster Arcade and Cash's department store had also been set ablaze, but hope of saving either soon evaporated as it became clear the fire had taken too strong a hold on both buildings.

On the opposite side of the river, the City Hall and Carnegie Free Library were burning furiously by 4 a.m. Firemen stationed at the City Hall had observed petrol tins being carried into the building, followed by a series of loud explosions.

Throughout the course of the night, the Cork firemen were constantly harassed and intimidated by the Black and Tans and Auxiliaries while trying to tackle the massive conflagration in the city centre, which prevented them from extinguishing the flames. About thirty policemen, a head constable and three sergeants continually turned off the hydrant, preventing the firemen from extinguishing the fire at the City Hall. The firemen were eventually forced to give up and brought their equipment to the fires in Georges Street (now Oliver Plunkett Street). At about 5.40 the clock tower of City Hall collapsed into the now largely gutted building and shortly afterwards only smouldering ruins remained of the once impressive building.

In the reports given to the Irish Labour Party's commissioners, as they compiled the evidence that would be published in *Who Burnt Cork City?*, many firemen spoke of being fired on as they tried to extinguish various blazes. Some attempting to leave the Sullivan's Quay station were driven back inside when they were shot at from across the river by Auxiliaries on Grand Parade. The fire brigade ambulance was also fired on and a bullet mark was later found just behind where the driver was sitting. Another fireman was tackling the fire at the Lee Boot Company in Patrick Street when three shots were fired at him. An auxiliary fireman, escorted by the military to

Brooke Hughes photographic establishment was situated above The Munster Arcade, one of the first buildings to be entirely consumed by the flames. (Author's collection)

# SCANNELL & DOWLING,

## Provision Merchants

### And POULTRY DEALERS,

## 16, Winthrop Street, CORK.

(Late of Russell & Son, Prince's St., Cork.)

An advertisement for Scannell & Dowling Provision Merchants and Poultry Dealers, another premises destroyed by fire off the main thoroughfare of Patrick Street. (Author's collection)

a fire in Merchant Street, was wounded in his right hip when he was fired on, and a second, who was ex-army himself, was shot at twice by a drunken officer of the Gordon Highlanders while working on Grant's. Another of the firemen working on Grant's was wounded in the right hand and left ear and had to be taken to the North Infirmary.

The best contemporary report of the progression of the fire throughout the evening and night of 11–12 December, and the difficulties faced by the men trying to fight it, comes from Superintendent Alfred Hutson, written just four days later:

## Official Report of the Superintendent of the City of Cork Fire Brigade

(December 15, 1920)

Incendiary Fires. Explosives Used. Hose Cut. Firemen Fired Upon. Military Refused Fire Appliances.

(Captain Hutson is an Englishman.)

The Right Hon. the Lord Mayor of Cork.

Sir, – In reference to the fires which occurred in the city on Saturday night, December 11, 1920, I beg to report as follows:–

A. – At 10.30 p.m. I received a call to Messrs. A. Grant and Co., Patrick Street, whose extensive premises were on fire. I found that the fire had gained considerable headway and the flames were coming through the roof. I got three lines of hose to work – one in Mutton Lane and two in Market Lane, intersecting passages on either side of these premises. With a good supply of water we were successful in confining the fire to Messrs. Grant's Patrick Street premises, and prevented its spread to that portion running to the Grand Parade from Mutton Lane, which we saved, except with slight damage, the adjacent premises of Messrs. Hackett (jeweller) and Haynes (jeweller). The Market – a building mostly of timber – to the rear of Messrs. Grants was found to be in great danger. If this building became involved a conflagration would ensue with which it would be almost impossible to cope. Except for only a few minor outbreaks in the roof we were successful in saving the Market and also other valuable premises in Mutton Lane.

B. – During the above operations I received word from the Town Clerk that the Munster Arcade was on fire. This was about 11.30 p.m. I sent all the men and appliances available to contend with it. Shortly after I got word that Messrs. Cash's premises were on fire. I shortened down hose at Mutton Lane and sent all available stand-pipes, hose, &c., and men to contend with this fire. I found both the Munster Arcade and Messrs. Cash's well alight from end to end, with no prospect of saving either, and the fire spreading rapidly to the adjoining property. The area involved in these two fires was very large and embraced many valuable and extensive premises.

C. – All the hydrants and mains that we could possibly use were brought to bear upon the flames and points were selected where the fire may be possibly checked and our efforts concentrated there. The General Post Office fire appliances were brought out and did good service in and around Winthrop Street, Robert Street, &c. I regret to state that I found this new hose had been cut in several places whilst in the streets and was of no further use. It was not until about 8 a.m. when I may state that the whole of the numerous points to which the flames had reached were partially under control.

D – About 4 a.m., I was informed that the Municipal Buildings were on fire. Knowing that there was a practical man with half a dozen men under his control there I had some confidence that they would be able to deal effectively with the fire as had already been done on three previous occasions. I very much regret, however, that the incendiaries were successful in driving my men out of the buildings and also from the Carnegie Free Library.

E. – I continued to do my best to confine the fires to the numerous streets off Patrick Street up to 10.30 a.m. on Sunday morning, having been on duty from 7 a.m. on the previous day.

Mr Delaney, city engineer, kindly came to my assistance and provided supervision of the men at work at the various points required.

F. – In connection with the fires at Dillon's Cross I wish to say that on receipt of the call for that fire I got in touch with the military at Victoria Barracks and asked them to take their hose reel and stand-pipes at the barrack gate down at once as I had been called to Grant's fire in Patrick Street, but they took no notice of my request. At the Patrick Street fires it is remarkable that the military never brought any fire appliances whatever – as they had done on nearly all previous occasions up to the last few months. I must say prior to these incendiary fires the military frequently rendered us valuable assistance not only in keeping the streets clear but also in extinguishing the fires. The statements of the two firemen working at Scully O'Connell's fire indicate the general position of the military on this occasion.

G. – I have no hesitation in stating I believe all the above fires were incendiary fires and that a considerable amount of petrol or some such inflammable spirit was used in one and all of them. In some cases explosives were also used and persons were seen to go into and come out of the structures after breaking an entrance into same, and in some cases that I have attended the people have been brought out of their houses and detained in by-lanes until the fire had gained great headway. I have some of the petrol tins left behind in my possession.

I remain, Your obedient servant,

ALFRED J. HUTSON.

Hutson was Cork's fire superintendent from 1891 to 1928. Born in Surrey on 14 April 1849, he joined the merchant navy at the age of fifteen and rose through the ranks to become a warrant officer by the age of twenty-two. On 20 September 1871 he applied for a position in the Metropolitan Fire Brigade Headquarters in Watling Street, London. He was accepted as a recruit under the tutelage of Captain Shaw and later held posts in various Metropolitan Fire Brigade stations, as well as being fire engineer to the General Steam Navigation Company.

**One of the few building façades still standing, Sunner's Chemist is like a landmark amidst the rubble of the city centre. According to one eyewitness, 'About three or four petrol tins were on the ground opposite Sunner's door … The lamp was lighting over our door and we could see things plainly.' (Courtesy of Mercier Archive)**

# A LINK WITH OLD CORK

The portion of an old Cork chimney-piece depicted in the above plate forms an interesting link with the days of the Irish Baronial residences or castles.

This architectural fragment was a portion of Skiddy's Castle, which was built in 1445, and can be distinctly seen in the front wall of our premises North Main Street. It is an interesting relic of the Tudor period, and bears the date 1597.

In 1891 he applied successfully for the position of fire superintendent in Cork and his second-in-command was Mark Wickham, brigade foreman. Hutson soon made his mark and many letters praising the brigade for prompt and courageous attendance at fires in the 1890s are recorded.

The employment of auxiliary firemen, the placing of fire extinguishers in police stations and the creation of fire escapes in buildings around the city, the building of a new fire station and sub-stations, supplying and checking of hydrants, and improved telephone connections all contributed to the development of the fire service in the city. Hutson played a leading role in all of this. His other duties included inspections under the Factories Act and recommending renewals of licences for the storage of petrol, providing an ambulance service and attending fires outside the city boundary when requested. However, no amount of pre-planning could have prepared the Cork fire brigade for what it faced that evening.

An interesting contrast to the detailed report given by Captain Hutson is provided by the military's official daily curfew report on the state of Cork city covering the period 10 p.m. on Saturday to 5.30 a.m. on Sunday by Major F. R. Eastwood of the 17th Infantry Brigade:

1) Three arrests were made.

2) At 22.00 hours, Grant & Co., in Patrick Street, was found to be on fire. Warning was at once sent to all fire brigades.

3) At about 00.30 hours. Cash & Co. and the Munster Arcade were reported on fire.

*Opposite:*
**John Daly was a whiskey blender who was also renowned for creating the famous Cork mineral Tanora. His premises on Caroline Street at the rear of Cash's was destroyed. (Author's collection)**

4) At 05.30 hours the majority of the troops were withdrawn, and the remainder at 08.00 hours.

5) Explosions were heard at 00.15 hours, but were not located. No shots were fired by the troops.

F. R. Eastwood, *Major*,

Brigade Major, 17th Infantry Brigade.

Cork 12.12.20.

He almost makes it sound like a quiet night! However, a very different and also very illuminating military perspective on the night appeared in a statement given by Captain P. H. Hudson of the 2nd Battalion, Hampshire Regiment, to the Strickland Enquiry:

The total strength of the curfew troops which left Victoria Barracks at the curfew hour on 11 December was 6 officers and 52 other ranks, exclusive of the searchlight and armoured car. It was about 01.00 hours when I ordered the armoured car to fire on any parties of the Auxiliary police found in the streets who were out of control. I issued this order on my own initiative. I did not repeat these orders to my own patrol as I did not consider it advisable as a battle would inevitably ensue, and my patrol was not strong enough. Before leaving barracks, I was told by the Brigade Major in written instructions to expect ambushes by the rebel forces, one in the neighbourhood of Barrack Street, and the other in the north-west area. In consequence, I had to bear in mind during the night the possibility of attack by such rebel forces.

This picture of the Auxiliaries is a very different one than would be painted in official reports after the fact.

Fire was not the only problem facing the businessmen of Cork throughout the night of 11–12 December. Some members of the British forces took advantage of the chaos to line their own pockets, with Mangan's, Egan's and Hilser's, Cork's premier jewellery shops, all extensively looted during the night. One eyewitness account given to the Irish Labour Party commissioners stated that they saw a number of men force their way into Mangan's. When they came out the witness noted that some were wearing police uniforms, and all appeared to be 'heavily laden' with loot from the store. Later, another set of looters visited Mangan's and left 'with pockets bulging'. Numerous eyewitness reports talk of men in various kinds of uniforms looting shops. Men's outfitters were another popular target and there are several descriptions of raids on this type of premises. Auxiliaries, Black and Tans and members of the regular RIC were seen on King Street, 'laden with suitcases, travelling rugs, coats, and hats'. Not surprisingly several public houses were also looted and large quantities of whiskey and brandy stolen, helping fuel the general drunkenness noted amongst the crown forces as the night wore on. In fact some of them lost their ill-gotten gains in the need for a drink. One eyewitness in the Irish Labour Party report stated that 'One policeman with a Scotch or Northern accent left a large Christmas stocking behind him on the counter, and another policeman with a like accent left a pair of underpants.' These articles, at least, were later returned to their rightful owners, Power Bros drapers and tailors.

Owing to the very extensive conflagrations and the scale of the havoc caused to the city, it soon became clear that it would be impossible for the Cork Fire Brigade to deal with the escalating situation on its own. Lord Mayor O'Callaghan sent out a call for assistance to other cities in the hope that reinforcements could help prevent the spread of the fires and more widespread damage and destruction. Captain Myers and seven firemen travelled from Dublin with their large motor fire engine, which was transported to Cork by special train. The Limerick and Waterford Fire Brigades also responded to the call.

Throughout Sunday night and the following days the firemen from Cork and, when they arrived, those from Dublin, Waterford and Limerick, assisted by many willing helpers, fought to bring the flames in a number of buildings under control, prevent other establishments catching fire and finally extinguish completely the smouldering remains of the city centre. The Freeman's Journal, quoted in Pat Poland's Firecall, later reported that when he arrived from Dublin at 2 a.m. on the morning of Monday 13 December, Captain Myers did not think that Cork could be saved, as 'When they arrived they were in a sea of darkness and they suddenly emerged in a sea of flame.' Six streets were apparently still ablaze at this point. In his report, Myers paid tribute to the Cork firemen who had been at their posts since the start of the burning: 'I saw the brave boys still playing the hoses on the burning buildings. It makes me cry to see such a scene of destruction. The only way to bring it home to the people of Dublin is to say that Cork is even worse than O'Connell Street, Abbey Street and the adjoining streets after Easter week.' Even at this late stage the firemen were still not safe from the threat of violence from out-of-control policemen. At 1.30 a.m. on Monday 13 December a fireman working the boiler of a fire engine on Merchants Quay was hit by a bullet in the nose and was taken by ambulance to the South Infirmary Hospital.

The fire brigade worked for a week after the burning to damp down the fires completely. Once they were out, the enormous task of clearing away the debris in the widely devastated areas began. Due to the extent of the devastation it was clear that this process would take some time. In the meantime rope chains were placed around many streets, surrounding the ruined and wrecked buildings. The public were ordered, for their own safety, to stay behind these chains as the dangerous work of clearing the ruins started.

From Monday 13 December, the work of some of the firemen was confined to removing debris, securing areas for traffic and demolishing portions of dangerous structures. City Hall and the Carnegie Free Library, which had been extensively damaged, attracted a lot of attention from the public, and it was possible to salvage some important documents held in the strong safes in City Hall. Little could be saved from the library, other than the books that were out on loan.

On Monday afternoon, the temporarily suspended city tram service partially resumed, when some trams began running on the Western Road route. The Patrick Street, Blackpool and Summerhill routes were still out of action. The failure of the gas supply caused by the conflagration affected the restricted volume of business that could be transacted that afternoon. Fortunately, by the evening the Cork Gas Company managed to restore the supply of gas to the city and suburbs.

Not long after the fires were extinguished, representatives from numerous building firms started to busily inspect ruined premises in the city. City Engineer J. F. Delaney supervised the necessary removal of dangerous walls that had been left standing amongst the ruins. It would take many months before all the debris in Cork city centre was finally cleared.

**Hosing the façade of The New York House on Sunday morning. This establishment sold handmade cigarettes and Indian cigars. (Courtesy of Mercier Archive)**

The fires are still smoking in the ruins in this photograph. According to an eyewitness for the Labour Party of the events of that night, they heard 'a voice, in a decided English accent, say "We'll finish — old Cork", and immediately afterwards another bomb exploded'. (Courtesy of Mercier Archive)

# J. Waters & Sons
### LIMITED.

## Oil, Color, Glass, Lead, and Drug Merchants,

## DISPENSING CHEMISTS.

## Picture Frame Manufacturers

### IMPORTERS OF PICTURE MOULDINGS, PHOTOGRAVURES AND OLEOGRAPHS.

## British & Foreign Glass, Sheets & Squares. Plate, Sheet, and Mirror Glass.

## Shop Mirrors, Framed & Unframed

### SUPPLIED AT SHORTEST NOTICE.

## 4, Winthrop Street & Winthrop Lane
## CORK.

J. Waters & Sons, another old Cork firm that was burned out, specialised in glass and was also a dispensing chemist. (Author's collection)

*Right:*

The start of the clean-up. A letter written by an Auxiliary and quoted in the Labour Party report said of his comrades, 'In all my life and in all the tales of fiction I have read I have never experienced such orgies of murder, arson and looting as I have witnessed during the past sixteen days with the RIC Auxiliaries.' (Author's collection)

After Cork Fire, Dec. 1920. Patrick Street.

*Below:*

A view of the opposite side of Patrick Street from the ruins of Cook Street. (Courtesy of Cork Public Museum)

Patrick Street after Cork Fire, December, 1920.

RUINS OF FORREST'S EGAN'S & ARCADE.

were in an extremely hazardous condition and in danger of imminent collapse. (Author's collection)

*Opposite bottom:*
The ruins of Forrest's and Egan's. According to a Labour Party eyewitness, 'A little after midnight, Egan's and Forrest's were well ablaze, and the windows of the Victoria Hotel … were beginning to catch fire.' (Author's collection)

*Below:*
The ruins of The Munster Arcade. According to an eyewitness who spoke to the Labour Party commissioners, 'The Munster Arcade, Cash's and adjoining property were a mass of flames … We noticed a few Auxiliaries with Glengarry caps, holding revolvers, walking about. … [A Black and Tan] said to us "Clear off the streets, as I don't know what the Auxiliaries might do; some of their comrades were shot".' (Courtesy of the *Irish Examiner*)

Firemen are still attempting to put out the dying fires, as the clean-up gains momentum. The Labour Party report notes that one Auxiliary asked, 'And why are such murderous incendiaries not censured? Perhaps because they are a convenient instrument for torturing the Irish people.' (Author's collection)

*Left:*
An Egan's Christmas 1920 advertisement showing their unrivalled selection of jewellery. Unfortunately this shop did not survive the conflagration. (Author's collection)

*Below:*
There was little for the men and boys who picked through the devastation to find, as little of value was left. (Author's collection)

NS OF CASH'S LONDON HOUSE & O'SULLIVAN'S.

*Above:*
Clearly the remains of some of the buildings were extremely dangerous, but this did not prevent people from scavenging in the rubble. One Labour Party eyewitness reported that on the night of the burning a man in an RIC uniform shouted at him: 'At your peril don't turn the hose on that fire. Let it blaze.' (Author's collection)

*Below:*
The well-established firm of R. & J. McKechnie Ltd had acquired the Dartry Dye Co. some months before the conflagration, but was obliterated by the fire. (Author's collection)

The devastation on Maylor Street. A Labour Party eyewitness said, 'I saw a group of police, numbering five or six, in uniform and with rifles, go down Maylor Street ... A few minutes afterwards I heard an explosion in the direction of Maylor Street.' (Author's collection)

RUINS OF GRANT'S & HAYNES'S.

RUINS FROM WINTHROP STREET TO MAYLOR STREET.

*Opposite top:*
A fireman hoses down the smouldering ruins of Grant's and Haynes'. (Author's collection)

*Opposite bottom:*
One fireman said in his evidence to the Labour Party commissioners, 'I brought my fire-reel into Winthrop Street, and as we were coming round five or six Auxiliaries with tasselled caps at the corner of the Post Office fired a volley towards us. … A bullet grazed my leg and made a slight wound.' (Author's collection)

*Below:*
Burned-out buildings on Robert Street. According to a Labour Party eyewitness, 'Looking out, I saw that the Munster Arcade had been set on fire and that the flames had in fact reached the Robert Street side in the space of a few minutes.' (Author's collection)

The only known picture of the burning of the city taken at night. (Author's collection)

## ESTABLISHED 1835.

# W. MARSH & SONS

### Auctioneers and Valuers, Cattle Salesmen, etc. ::

## 70 South Mall & Copley St.
### CORK.

Telephone No. 347.   Repository Telephone No. 488.
Telegrams : "MARSH, CORK."

Valuations for Probate, Fire Insurance, &c.

## WEEKLY AUCTION
OF
## DAIRY and STORE CATTLE and SHEEP
AT THE
### Repository, Copley Street, Cork, every Saturday.

Special Store Cattle Sales Periodically.

Marsh & Sons Auctioneers, established in 1835, whose South Mall premises were destroyed by fire even though this was quite a distance from the main fires on Patrick Street. (Author's collection)

The clock tower of City Hall, which collapsed into the ruins. The clock had long been a target for British forces as is evident from the bullet holes in its face from earlier in 1920. (Courtesy of Mercier Archive)

The limestone façade is all that was left of City Hall. A wooden hoarding was erected to keep people away from the ruins at the far end. (Courtesy of Mercier Archive)

Carnegie Free Library, Cork.

**Above:**

A commercial postcard of the Carnegie Free Library before its destruction. This fine library had a collection of about 15,000 books. (Author's collection)

**Right:**

The Carnegie Free Library official bookmark for 1909. Advertising spaces could be purchased from Messrs Stanley Russell & Co., London Bridge. (Author's collection)

*Top left:*
The philanthropist Andrew Carnegie, who provided the funds to build the Carnegie Free Library. Opened in 1905, the library's destruction in 1920 left Cork city without a public library service until 1924. (Courtesy of the Library of Congress, LC-USZ62–120152)

*Centre left:*
James Wilkinson was the librarian in charge of the Carnegie Free Library until its complete destruction. (Courtesy of Cork City Library)

*Below:*
The ruins of City Hall. According to Captain Hutson's report, he initially had confidence that his men would be able to deal with the fire there, but 'the incendiaries were successful in driving my men out of the buildings'. (Courtesy of the *Irish Examiner*)

*Above:*

People going about their business with the ruins of the Carnegie Free Library in the background – the roof and interior had been totally destroyed. (Author's collection)

*Right:*

The Carnegie Free Library ticket which was attached to all the books for borrowing in the library. (Author's collection)

Leabarlann Carneiġi, Corcaiġe.

IASAĊT.

Ar orcailt óna 10 ɣo oʈi a 9.
Ar oúnaó Oé Céaoaoin óna 1.

Books must be protected from soiling and from every other kind of injury. Should any damage be observed it should be at once pointed out to the Librarian.

Books should, if possible, be changed by borrowers personally. If a messenger be employed the borrower is responsible.

Immediate notice is to be given to the Librarian of loss of book or of ticket, and also of change of address.

*In the event of any infectious disease occurring in any house where there are Library Books, such books must not be returned to the Library, but handed over to an officer of the Sanitary Authority to be disinfected or destroyed. Until such house is declared free from infection by the Sanitary Officer no books will be issued to any persons residing therein. Any person neglecting to comply with this instruction shall be liable in respect of each offence to a penalty not exceeding Forty Shillings. (" The Public Health Acts Amendment Act, 1907,.")*

CLASS.................... ACC. No....................

*Right:*
A rare survivor: one of the books which was rescued, water-stained, from the Carnegie. (Author's collection)

*Below:*
Members of the Cork City Fire Brigade. Captain Myers of the Dublin Fire Brigade paid tribute to the manner in which the Cork firemen stayed at their posts during the burnings despite the evident danger. (Courtesy of Pat Poland)

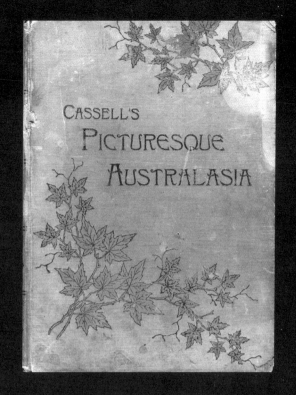

*Above left:* Captain Alfred Hutson, whose brave firemen prevented many of the fires from spreading, saving many buildings from destruction. (Courtesy of Pat Poland)

*Above right:* A horse-drawn hose reel known as a jumper. (Courtesy of Pat Poland)

*Below:* The Cork Corporation horse-drawn steam engine and the Dublin Fire Brigade's modernised motor vehicle draw water from the River Lee. (Courtesy of Pat Poland)

The Dublin Fire Brigade who came to help put out the fires are pictured outside the remaining Façade of the Lee Cinema on Winthrop Street as an RIC man and crowds look on. (Courtesy of *Irish Examiner*)

*Below:*

A fireman among the ruins. In relation to the aftermath of the burning, an American called Emil Pezolt told the American Commission that 'If any of you saw San Franscisco after the earthquake, you know how Patrick Street looked.' (Author's collection)

*Opposite:*

The National Bank on the South Mall, the manager of which was so nervous about the general lawlessness by British forces that he issued a memo to staff outlining what to do in the event of a repeat of the burnings. (Author's collection)

*Below:*

The National Bank memo, sent to all cashiers on 13 December, patently blamed the Auxiliary forces for the recent outrages. (Author's collection)

MEMORANDUM.

13 DEC 1920      19___

FROM

The National Bank Limited,      To All Cashiers

CORK BRANCH

Re. the recent outrages against property &c. carried out by local auxiliary forces. Should there be a repetition of lawlesness by the above mentioned the following precautions are to be observed: I. Porters to lock all doors and escort remaining customers to rear of premises. 2. Cashier tills to be secured and counter staff to follow to the rear and remain thus until deemed safe by senior staff to reopen for business. Your cooperation in this matter is essential.

MANAGER.

The façade of The Stags Head bar and billiard rooms on Maylor Street after the fire. (Courtesy of Mercier Archive)

# BUSINESS PREMISES
# DESTROYED

Following the destruction of the night of 11–12 December, over 600 claims for compensation were lodged with Cork Corporation. Unfortunately very little information exists relating to the trades and professions located over the main establishments that were destroyed or badly damaged, or for smaller shops and premises located in the side streets. The following information has been put together from *Guy's Directories* for 1918–21, *The Cork Examiner* of 14 December 1920 and the report on the conflagration carried out by Cork Corporation's city engineer, J. F. Delaney.

## Patrick Street

(Fire starts at no. 12, Patrick Street; all buildings before no. 12 and on the opposite side of Merchant Street not destroyed.)

| | | |
|---|---|---|
| O'Sullivan, J. (New York Hse) | Tobacconist | 12 Patrick Street |
| Clegg, F. J. | Teeth Specialist | 12 Patrick Street |
| Irish Drapers | Assistants Benefit Assoc. | 12 Patrick Street |
| Woulfe, J. | Outfitter | 13 Patrick Street |
| McDonnell & Son | Hairdressers | 13 Patrick Street |
| Roches Stores | Drapers | 14–15 Patrick Street |
| Archer, James | Engraver | 14 Patrick Street |

| | | |
|---|---|---|
| Belas, John G. | Commission agent | 14 Patrick Street |
| Harte, Mrs | Dressmaker | 14 Patrick Street |
| Lee Boot Co. | Manufacturer | 16 Patrick Street |
| O'Shea | Dressmaker | 16 Patrick Street |
| Scully, O'Connell | Children's outfitters | 17 Patrick Street |
| O'Donoghue, Miss | Professor of music | 17 Patrick Street |

(Maylor Street intersects 17 and 18 Patrick Street)

| | | |
|---|---|---|
| Cash & Co. | Drapers & warehouse | 18–21 Patrick Street |

(Winthrop Street intersects 21 and 22 Patrick Street)

| | | |
|---|---|---|
| Thompson & Co. | Hosiery & Fancy warehouse | 22 Patrick Street |
| Cudmore, R. | Fruiter | 22a Patrick Street |
| Burton Ltd | Men's outfitters | 23 Patrick Street |
| Saxone & Sorosis | Shoe company | 24 Patrick Street |
| McKechnie, R. & J. | Dyers | 25 Patrick Street |
| Cahalane, S. P. | Watchmaker & jeweller | 25 Patrick Street |
| O'Regan & Co. | Hosiers | 26 Patrick Street |
| Carey & Walsh | Hairdressers | 26 Patrick Street |

(Robert Street intersects 26 and 28 Patrick Street (there is no No. 27 listed in *Guy's Directory*))

| | | |
|---|---|---|
| The Munster Arcade | Drapers & warehouse | 28–30 Patrick Street |
| Brooke Hughes | Photographer | 28 Patrick Street |
| Sunner, R. | Chemist | 31 Patrick Street |
| W. Egan & Sons | Silversmith | 32 Patrick Street |
| American Studio | Photographer | 32 Patrick Street |
| Forrest & Sons | Silk Merchants | 33–34 Patrick Street |

The building with the striped panel is the remains of the Lee Cinema, which was adjacent to Cash & Co. According to a Labour Party eyewitness, 'At 1 a.m. we left our premises, as we could see that the fire from Cash's was coming nearer and we could see people from adjoining premises clearing their premises and leaving them for safety.' (Author's collection)

(Cook Street intersects 34 and 35 Patrick Street. The Victoria Hotel on the corner of Patrick Street and Cook Street was not burned down. Only minor smoke damage was sustained due to the hotel having its own fire equipment. From here there was a break in the destruction, which started again after Mutton Lane, which intersects 50 and 51 Patrick Street.)

| | | |
|---|---|---|
| Haynes & Son | Watchmakers | 51 Patrick Street |
| Ryng, John | Vintner | 51 Patrick Street |
| Nagle, John | Victualler | 51 Patrick Street |
| A. Grant & Co. | Drapers | 52–54 Patrick Street |

*Little remains of Grant's Department Store, just some cast-iron pillars and debris. (Author's collection)*

| | | |
|---|---|---|
| Hackett, J. | Jeweller | 55 Patrick Street |
| McTighe | Tobacconist | 55 Patrick Street |

## Premises Destroyed on Patrick Street by Trade

| | |
|---|---|
| Chemist | 1 |
| Commission agent | 1 |
| Drapers establishments | 4 |
| Drapers association | 1 |
| Dressmakers | 2 |
| Dyers | 1 |

| | |
|---|---|
| Engravers | 1 |
| Fruiters | 1 |
| Hairdressers | 2 |
| Hosiery | 2 |
| Jewellers & watchmakers | 4 |
| Outfitters | 2 |
| Professor of music | 1 |
| Photo studios | 2 |
| Shoe shops | 2 |
| Silk merchants | 1 |
| Teeth specialists | 2 |
| Tobacconists | 2 |
| Vintners | 1 |
| Victuallers | 1 |
| | |
| Total | 34 |

Egan & Sons was one of the jewellers destroyed on Patrick Street. (Author's collection)

## Side Street Premises Destroyed by Fire

### Merchant Street

| | | |
|---|---|---|
| Dolphin Bar | Vintner & billiard rooms | 25 Merchant Street |
| O'Sullivan, J. | New York House wholesale | 25 Merchant Street |

### Maylor Street

| | | |
|---|---|---|
| O'Shea, Miss | Dress & mantle rooms | 22 Maylor Street |
| Dixon, J. | Tea agent | 22 Maylor Street |
| Steele, J. | Commercial agent | 22 Maylor Street |
| Lee Boot Co. | Shoe shop | 22 Maylor Street |

| | | |
|---|---|---|
| Walsh, Robert | Vintner | 23 Maylor Street |
| Lee Boot Co. | Factory store | 23 Maylor Street |
| The Stags Head | Bar & billiard rooms | 24 Maylor Street |
| Cash & Co. | Upholstery warehouse | 24–25 Maylor Street |
| Ryan, J. | Paper merchant | 26 Maylor Street |
| Sullivan, D. | Brush maker | 27 Maylor Street |
| Creen & Co. | Corn merchant | 28 Maylor Street |

## Winthrop Street[1]

| | | |
|---|---|---|
| Lee Cinema | Picture house | 1 & 2 Winthrop Street |
| Tomkins & Sons | Wine & spirits merchant | 19 Winthrop Street |
| Tyler & Sons | Boot store | 20 Winthrop Street |
| McNie, S. | Jewellery manufacturer | Winthrop Chambers |
| McAuliffe, J. | Commercial agent | Winthrop Chambers |
| Treacy, E. | Millers agent | Winthrop Chambers |
| Foley, M. | Commercial agent | Winthrop Chambers |
| O'Keene, Mrs | Dressmaker & milliner | Winthrop Chambers |
| Long, F. | Commercial agent | Winthrop Chambers |
| Murphy, M. | Fruiter & confectioner | 21 Winthrop Street |

## Robert Street

| | | |
|---|---|---|
| The Munster Arcade | Laundry | 3 Robert Street |
| Shandon Printing Works | Printers | 4–6 Robert Street |
| McKetterick, S. V. | Bookbinding establishment | 7 Robert Street |
| Mulcahy, D. | Ironworks | 8 Robert Street |
| Hagan, Maurice | Barber | 9 Robert Street |

---

1   Winthrop Chambers was either between or above nos 20 and 21 Winthrop Street.

Ladies' outfitters Cummins & Co. did not escape the indiscriminate devastation of property on Winthrop Street. (Author's collection)

## Cook Street

| Noonan, Patrick | Vintner | 1–2 Cook Street |
|---|---|---|
| Woods, E. | Wine merchant | 3 Cook Street |
| Metropole Hotel | Stockrooms | 3 Cook Street |
| Cashman & Co. | Grocers | 4 Cook Street |
| O'Connor, P. | Restaurant | 5 Cook Street |
| Martin, Michael | Fruiter | 6 Cook Street |

## Georges Street (now Oliver Plunkett Street)

| O'Shea, Miss | Tobacconist | 34 Georges Street |
|---|---|---|
| Herlihy, Miss | News depot | 35 Georges Street |
| The Munster Arcade | Cabinet factory | 36 Georges Street |
| Cahill, M. | Vintner | 37 Georges Street |
| Hoare, W. | Veterinary stables | Georges Street (no. unknown) |
| Ahern, K. | Vintner | 96 Georges Street |
| Bateman, C. | Boot factory | 97 Georges Street |

| Druce, F. | Blouse manufacturer | 97 Georges Street |
| O'Callaghan, H. | Vintner | 98 Georges Street |

(Robert Street intersects 98 and 99 Georges Street)

| The Munster Arcade | Rear of store | 99–101 Georges Street |
| Forde, Patrick | Vintner | 103 Georges Street |

## Premises Badly Damaged

| Nagle, J. | Victualler | 38 Georges Street |
| Fitzgerald, J. | Creamery | 104 Georges Street |
| O'Sullivan, J. | Chemist | 105 Georges Street |
| Cahill, N. | Tobacconist | 106 Georges Street |
| Ryan, James | Paper & twine stores | 21 Merchant Street |
| Cork Furniture Stores | Store | 22–24 Merchant Street |
| O'Sullivan, D. F. | Tea merchant | 15–17 Maylor Street |
| O'Sullivan, D. | Brush manufacturer | 18 Maylor Street |
| Molloy, Thomas | Lodging house | 19 Maylor Street |
| Clifford's | Private hotel | 30 Maylor Street |
| Ferguson, L. | Hairdresser | 3 Winthrop Street |
| Waters, J. J. | Oil & colour merchant | 4 Winthrop Street |
| Power Bros | Tailors & hatters | 5 Winthrop Street |
| Tierney, T. | Fancy fair | 15 Winthrop Street |
| Scannell & Dowling | Provisions merchant | 16 Winthrop Street |
| O'Shea, M. F. | Tobacconist | 16a Winthrop Street |
| Cummins & Co. | Ladies' outfitters | 17 Winthrop Street |
| Hanley & Sons | Victuallers | 17a Winthrop Street |
| Manley, Joshua | Provisions dealer | 18 Winthrop Street |
| Marsh, S. | Auctioneers | Morgan Street |

## Premises Wrecked and Looted

| | | |
|---|---|---|
| Buckley, P. D. | Tobacconist | 3 Grand Parade Buildings |
| Farmers Union | Rooms | Marlboro Street |
| *Irish Times* | Offices | 13 Marlboro Street |
| Y.M.C.A. | Hall | 11 Marlboro Street |
| Munster Type | Writing co. | 28 Marlboro Street |
| Kingston, J. | Vintner | 32 Marlboro Street |
| Wilson, D. | Painter | 33 Marlboro Street |
| Cohwie Bros | Provisions merchant | 82 Georges Street |
| Flynn, D. | Draper | 83 Georges Street |
| Tadman, F. V. | Hairdresser | 55 Georges Street |
| Murphy, Mrs | Tobacconist | 58 Georges Street |
| Griffin, Gerald | Boot Factory | 59 Georges Street |

The front page of *The Graphic* illustrated weekly newspaper of 18 December 1920 showing the stark remains of Sunner's Chemist. (Courtesy of Noel Scannell)

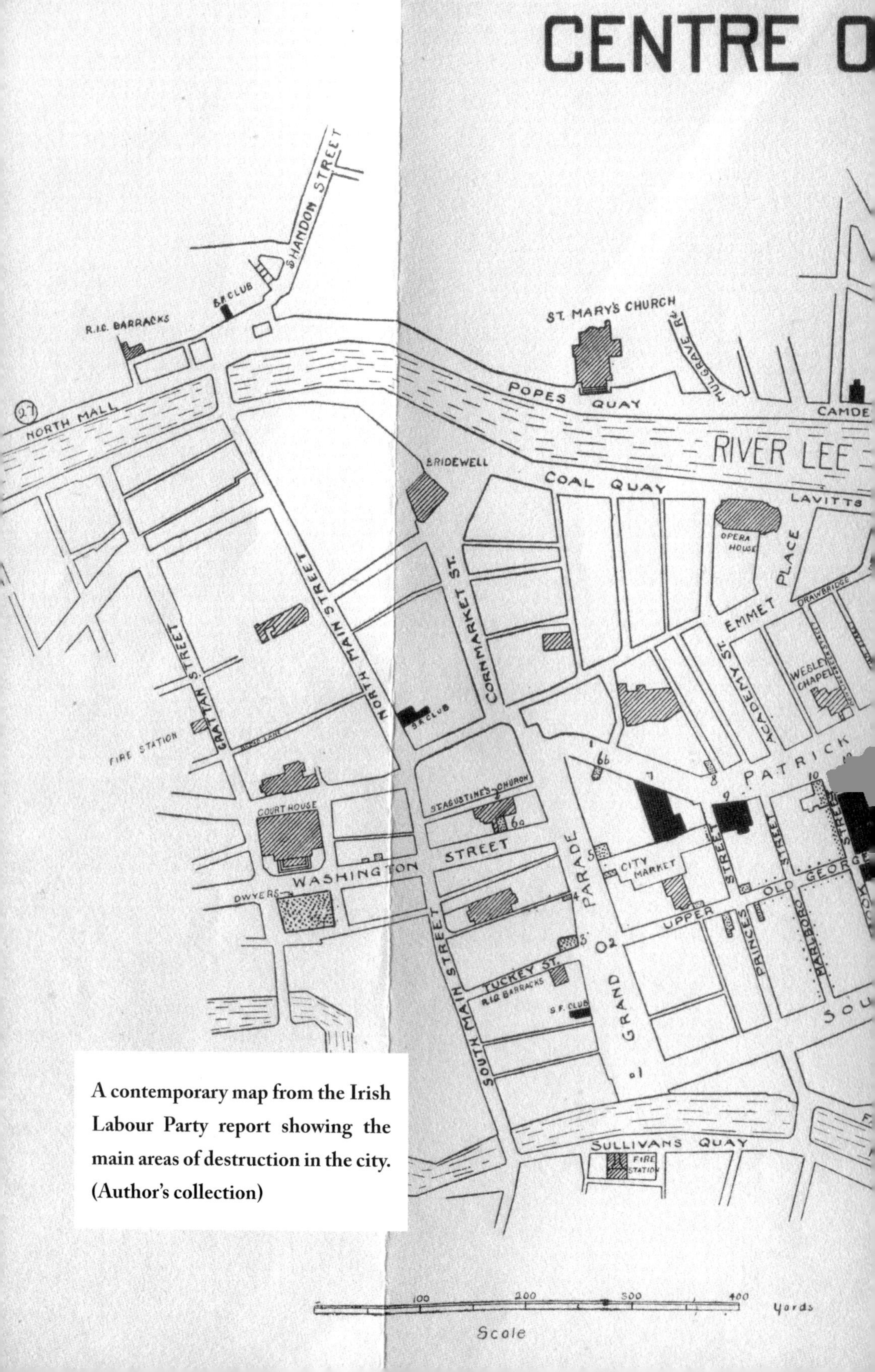

A contemporary map from the Irish Labour Party report showing the main areas of destruction in the city. (Author's collection)

SHANDON STREET

B.F. CLUB

R.I.C. BARRACKS

ST. MARY'S CHURCH

MULGRAVE RD.

NORTH MALL

POPES QUAY

CAMDE

RIVER LEE

BRIDEWELL

COAL QUAY

LAVITTS

OPERA HOUSE

CORNMARKET ST.

ACADEMY ST.

EMMET PLACE

DRAWBRIDGE

GRATTAN STREET

NORTH MAIN STREET

FIRE STATION

B.F. CLUB

66

7

8

PATRICK

9

10

COURT HOUSE

ST. AUGUSTINE'S CHURCH

6

WASHINGTON STREET

CITY MARKET

PRINCES STREET

OLD STREET

GEORGE

DWYERS

PARADE

8

UPPER

MARLBORO STREET

SOUTH MAIN STREET

TUCKEY ST.

R.I.C. BARRACKS

S.F. CLUB

GRAND

5

O 2

O 1

SOU

SULLIVANS QUAY

FIRE STATION

100    200    300    400    Yards

Scale

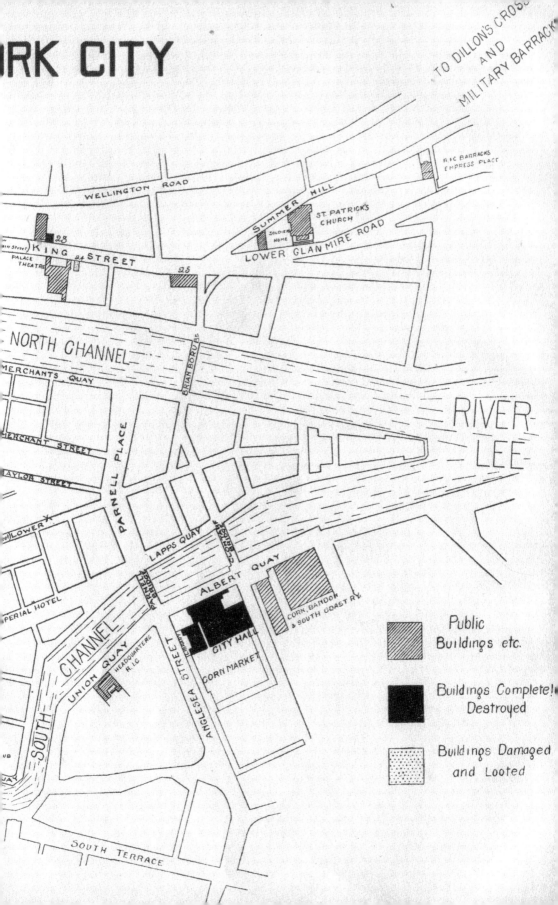

# RK CITY

TO DILLON'S CROSS
AND
MILITARY BARRACKS

R.I.C BARRACKS
EMPRESS PLACE

WELLINGTON ROAD

SUMMER HILL

ST. PATRICK'S
CHURCH

SOLDIERS
HOME

LOWER GLANMIRE ROAD

Main Street

KING 24 STREET

PALACE
THEATRE

23

25

NORTH CHANNEL

MERCHANTS QUAY

BRIAN BORU B?

RIVER-
LEE

MERCHANT STREET

AYLOR STREET

PARNELL PLACE

LOWER ✕

LAPPS QUAY

ALBERT QUAY

CORK, BANDON
& SOUTH COAST RY

IMPERIAL HOTEL

PARNELL BRIDGE

GEORGE ST

ANGLESEA STREET

LIBRARY

CITY HALL

CORN MARKET

SOUTH CHANNEL

UNION QUAY

HEADQUARTERS
R.I.C

Public
Buildings etc.

Buildings Completel
Destroyed

Buildings Damaged
and Looted

SOUTH TERRACE

People stare in disbelief at the ruins in the heart of their city centre. A sense of helplessness is apparent in this poignant image. (Courtesy of Mercier Archive)

# LOCAL REACTION
# TO THE BURNING

In the aftermath of the events of 11–12 December a number of eyewitness accounts were recorded that have survived to the present day and provide a vivid account of the destruction left behind by the fires. The following account, recorded in Healy's *The Story of Roches Stores*, starts with the recollections of William Roche, the founder of Roches Stores, which was destroyed by the fire:

'A friend cycled to my house at about 8 o'clock on the Sunday morning to tell me that "Cork was burned out and our premises had gone up with the rest".

'It was a really beautiful still frosty morning and I dressed at once and went into the City.

'Every place on the way in to town was strangely quiet, not a soul along the road. No traffic of any kind. Nothing moving and not a sound. When I came to the Free Library … I had the feeling of one in a dream. It was burning peaceably and one could say, beautifully. The flames were leaping upwards gracefully, making only a slight crackling noise occasionally. … I kept on my way and when I got opposite the building I saw two R.I.C. men chatting unconcernedly. One beckoned me to them and said, "Where are you going?" I said, "My name is Roche of Roches Stores and I understand our place is on fire and I am going into town to see what I can do." The same man, who was fully armed, thought for a moment and looking at me, gave me a gentle, not unfriendly, push and said, "Go on." It looked to me as, although not drunk, they had had a few drinks. Parnell Place, a wide street, was quite intact, but when I looked up Maylor Street, the strange gap which the destruction of a big slice of Patrick Street made, looked very startling. The

**Five lads look towards the camera as in the background Cork citizens examine the ruined remains of their city centre. (Author's collection)**

tall buildings which had been brought down let in so much light. I turned up a side street to our building and found that it was well alight and partly burned out. There were a few lookers-on and very soon some of our own people arrived and started to salvage some goods. This was done quietly and some strangers joined in the work.'

Pat Fitzgerald recalled, 'When I saw the premises next morning they were in flames. Our economical Calico Sign which had been tacked over the old name was blazing and the "London House" name stood out for some hours before the final destruction of the building.'

Roche continued his account: 'There were no fire engines or brigades available or no effort made to put out the fires. After half an hour or so I went into Patrick Street to see how things looked. There may have been about thirty people about at that time. Two military motor lorries dashed into Patrick Street from the King Street side, turned quickly round at Winthrop Street, and everyone ran for shelter not knowing the intentions of the military. Most of the people had time to go into side streets, but myself and a few others had not time so we stood against a shop window.

'The military fired a volley, I presume over our heads, but a few bullets shattered the window glass where I was standing. The lorries went off at a good speed and we were greatly relieved to see them go. ...

'We worked until about one o'clock at the salvaging and some of our men did very good work, especially at our safes. This work was done at some risk as walls were suddenly falling in in many places. We however saved all our leases and valuable documents.'

In the face of such devastation, it would have been understandable if Roche had just given up, but he and many of Cork's other businesspeople were determined to be back trading as soon as possible. Before rebuilding could commence, the debris of the fire had to be cleared and dangerous buildings and walls that were still standing demolished. The solution to this for Roche, who was one of the first to begin trading again, was to use his large existing warehouses, which had survived the conflagration, as a base from which to sell the stock he had managed to salvage from some of his Merchant Street stores. Other shop owners operated from temporary premises, such as Burton's, which traded for a while from 2 Patrick Street. Department stores such as Egan's, Cash's and The Munster Arcade commissioned builders to construct temporary wooden structures that they could trade from while their premises were being rebuilt. However, not surprisingly, the fire spelled the end for many businesses including Sunner's Chemist, the Lee Boot Company and the Old London House.

Although his business had survived the fire, being located well outside the city centre, Henry Ford received a report and a series of commissioned photographs of the destruction from his plant manager, Edward Grace. In the report Grace outlines the suspicions held by many about who was responsible for the destruction, as well as explaining the differences between the British forces to his American boss. He also reflects the fear that this was not the last arson attack the city might face:

In my cable I mentioned that the Auxiliary police and Black and Tans were alleged to be responsible for the burning of this large portion of the business district of Cork. Patrick

Street is the main thoroughfare of the city in which is situated all of the chief shops and several hundred families have been rendered homeless, who were residing in the upper storeys of the business houses. There seems to be little room left in the minds of the general public for doubt as to who are guilty of the burning and looting of this district.

In order to explain whom the Auxiliary police and Black and Tans are I wish to point out that up to the present time there have been four separate and distinct bodies in Ireland. First is the old RIC which is the ordinary police force and is composed of men, the greater numbers of whom are sound disciplined men. Second, the military who are here in thousands, fully equipped with armoured cars, tanks and all modern implements of war such as machine guns, pistols etc. Third, the Black and Tans, so called because of their wearing part soldiers' uniform and part police uniform. These are a band of men sent over from England and seem to be without any proper discipline. They have not been under the control of either the military or police but seem to carry on as they please without respect to any common decency. They have been alleged to have held up people to search them for political documents and in every instance where a man had money

*Above:*

A photograph showing the initial temporary enquiry huts erected by The Munster Arcade and William Egan and Sons. (Courtesy of Cork Public Museum)

*Opposite:*

Hackney cars outside the larger temporary business establishments constructed by The Munster Arcade and Egan's, enabling business to be carried on while compensation claims could be heard and plans for rebuilding made. (Courtesy of Mercier Archive)

*Above:*

The banner in this image advertises Roches Stores salvage sale. William Roche said, 'We were the first of the affected firms to get going and had a large calico sign erected on the Patrick Street ruins announcing "Salvage sale at Roches Stores".' (Author's collection)

*Opposite top:*

The temporary business constructed to enable Cash & Co. to conduct business. Some of the devastated businesses in the background would never be rebuilt. (Courtesy of Mercier Archive)

*Opposite bottom:*

R. Cudmore had a small temporary shop constructed on Patrick Street, while at No. 23 next door Burton's erected a sign directing customers to their temporary premises at No. 2 Patrick Street. (Courtesy of the *Irish Examiner*)

Evans' bookshop and stationers survived the fire, but on the opposite side of Merchant Street O'Sullivan's tobacconists and Roches Stores had to erect temporary structures. (Courtesy of the *Irish Examiner*)

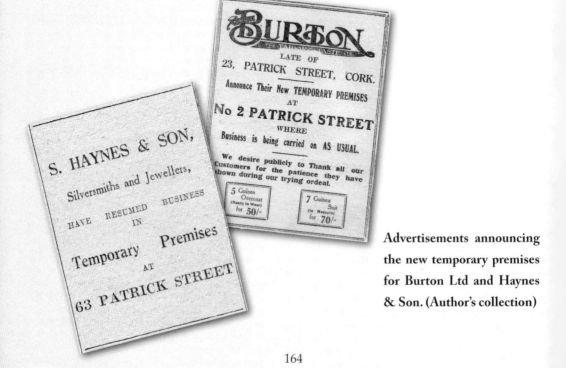

Advertisements announcing the new temporary premises for Burton Ltd and Haynes & Son. (Author's collection)

on him they relieved him of it. I have fortunately not had any encounter with any of them, but judging from the appearance of their faces, would say that they are a lot of the scum of England who have accepted the high pay offered to them to come here and do police duty, and are spending the same on booze that is when they are not able to steal it. The Auxiliary police are a body composed of ex-army officers recruited in England and while they are perhaps a little better type of men than the Black and Tans, seem to be uncontrolled and allowed to do as they please.

The burning of Cork is alleged to have been caused directly by a lorry full of Auxiliary police having been fired upon and sixteen of them wounded and one of them killed last Saturday evening, after which they all went mad and sought to destroy the city as a reprisal. As much as all sane thinking people deplore the act of cowardly murdering men from ambush, still one cannot imagine a modern government allowing its armed forces to take part in such an orgy of crime. As far as this works is concerned we are in no danger, firstly because it is owned by an American, and they fear that it might involve international complications, and next because we have about 1,500 men employed, and while so employed they have no time to think of other matters than their work. The only portions of our buildings that they could do any real damage through fire are the wooden buildings, which are covered well by insurance. I have been assured by the officer in charge here that we need have no fear from anything of this nature in the future.

However, despite the generally accepted belief amongst Cork citizens that the main culprits in the burning were the Auxiliaries and other British forces, the British government was not prepared to admit that its men were to blame.

*Above:*
Clearing the rubble. Lord Mayor O'Callaghan described the streets after the fire as 'a wilderness of ruin and debris'. (Courtesy of the *Irish Examiner*)

*Opposite top:*
This image of the devastation is one of those commissioned by Edward Grace. With the growing violence in Ireland during the War of Independence, Henry Ford was extremely worried about the safety of his factory on Centre Park Road. (Author's collection)

*Opposite bottom:*
Crowds assemble to view the devastation. In his report to the American Commission, O'Callaghan said, 'when you came to view the situation for the first time after the fire, on the following day, Patrick Street was really unrecognizable; you could not tell where the street was, where the splendid buildings had been.' (Courtesy of Mercier Archive)

Inevitably the sight of the city in pieces must have become accepted by the inhabitants. In this image two shawlies seem more interested in their conversation than the ruins they are passing. (Courtesy of the *Irish Examiner*)

As life returns to normal in Cork, a tram passes the burnt-out façade of City Hall. (Author's collection)

# BRITISH REACTION

The burning of Cork city and City Hall had to be blamed on somebody and a theory was quickly concocted to support a cover-up. When the events of that night were debated in the House of Commons, the chief secretary of Ireland, Sir Hamar Greenwood, and his allies, according to the Irish Labour Party report, initially blamed Sinn Féin extremists for the devastation. When questions were put to Greenwood by Liberal MP Lieutenant Commander Kenworthy, who asked whether it was true that three civilians had been killed and fire hoses had been cut by bayonets, Greenwood replied, 'There is not one atom of evidence that I know of to that effect.' According to the Labour Party report, the government apparently insisted that neither 'an ounce of ammunition, nor a gallon of petrol' was unaccounted for in any of the Cork barracks. This policy of denial and blame then went even further, maintaining that the crown forces had saved the city from destruction.

While these claims were clearly ridiculous, what followed defied all rational logic. On 14 December Greenwood insisted that the fire had started in City Hall and had spread from there to the business premises on Patrick Street. The previous day the *Daily Chronicle* had published a made-up map of Cork placing City Hall in the city centre to support this claim. This suggestion, of course, was quite ludicrous, as City Hall and the Carnegie Free Library were about a quarter of a mile on the other side of the river from Patrick Street, and moreover the timeline showed that buildings in Patrick Street were on fire before the conflagration in City Hall was started. The channel of the river and the intervening buildings would have made it impossible for a spark from City Hall to reach Patrick Street. Moreover, on the night in question, there was no wind and it was very calm, so much so that not even the other side of Patrick Street caught fire.

On 17 December *The Cork Examiner* noted that two members of the British Labour Party commission, Messrs Lawson and Lunn, had been sent to investigate the general cause and extent of the fires in Cork. Apparently news of the destruction of the city had not been a surprise to the commission. During a visit to the city on 6 December, the same two men had come to the conclusion that a serious outbreak of violence was probable as the increasing provocation by the Auxiliaries was likely to result in retaliation, or else that there would be a further outbreak of violence by the Auxiliaries themselves. The commissioners gathered evidence from witnesses revealing that shortly after 9 p.m. on the night of the burning the Auxiliaries and Black and Tans had intimidated citizens at revolver point, forcing them into their homes before curfew time. This had caused consternation, as people feared some sort of retaliation following the ambush at Dillon's Cross. The streets were soon deserted, enabling the work of destruction to commence unhindered.

Eyewitness statements unanimously said that forces of the crown were responsible for the fires in the city. Evidence was taken that members of the crown forces had entered buildings which afterwards were found to be on fire. The smashing of glass and doors was heard, as were explosions. Widespread looting by the Auxiliaries and Black and Tans was observed at different times by people living in the buildings.

Having visited the devastated city centre, the two commissioners stated that the newspaper accounts only conveyed a faint impression of the terrible havoc actually wrought on the city. It was clear that the crown forces had sought out the most valuable premises for destruction. Large department stores with massive shop frontages and other businesses had been reduced to smouldering ruins, with twisted iron girders the only remnants of the once fine buildings. The commissioners went on to report that, in monetary terms, rebuilding costs would run into millions of pounds. They stated that thousands of people were immediately unemployed, not including workers indirectly put out of work as a result of the fires.

The commissioners concluded that the majority of the fires took place before and during curfew hours when the majority of civilians were in their homes, that the choice of places set on fire indicated a preconceived plan of destroying the whole city centre and that, from the accounts of eyewitnesses, it was clear the police or the

**Chief Secretary Hamar Greenwood inspecting a group of RIC Auxiliaries. An Auxiliary who gave evidence to the Labour Party commissioners said of him, 'the burning and looting of Cork … We did it all right. Never mind how much the well-intentioned Hamar Greenwood would excuse us.' (Author's collection)**

Black and Tans were responsible for the destruction. The commissioners noted that they had not been granted a meeting with the Cork military authorities to hear the official information relating to the Dillon's Cross ambush and the city centre fires. As a result of their report, the British Labour Commission sent a resolution to the British prime minister asking 'that an independent and searching judicial enquiry be made immediately into the occurrences at Cork on Saturday last'.

An enormous amount of valuable property was mysteriously destroyed, thousands of people were now unemployed and hundreds homeless, and the citizens were left in a state of abject terror. Not surprisingly, the leaders of both Sinn Féin and the unionists in Cork threw their full political weight behind this demand for an impartial enquiry.

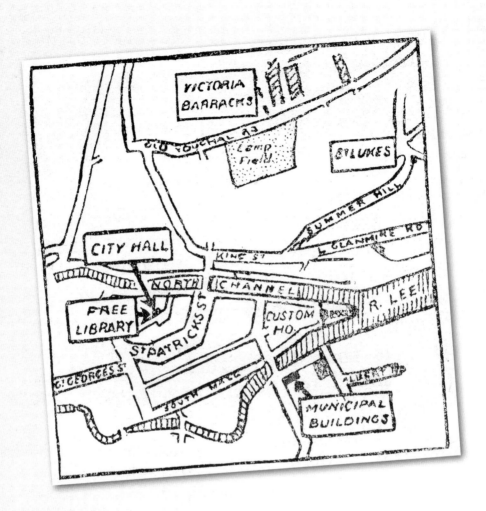

A fake map of Cork contrived to place City Hall and the Carnegie Free Library near Patrick Street in order to comply with the false theory that the fire spread from there to the city centre. (Author's collection)

On 13 December, Cork Corporation emphatically repudiated the suggestion that the city was burned by 'any section of its citizens'. It too demanded an impartial enquiry into the circumstances of the city's destruction. The Cork Chamber of Commerce supported this demand and expressed 'astonishment' at the chief secretary's cover-up of the facts. The Chamber of Commerce referred to a telegram sent by them to Greenwood on 29 November requesting immediate protection for citizens' property in view of incendiary fires occurring in Cork. The Cork Harbour Board and the Cork Employer's Federation added their voices to the demand that the government hold an immediate and searching enquiry into the circumstances of the burning. The British government, fearing the results of such an enquiry, decided instead to conduct an official military investigation, presided over by Major General Strickland, the commanding officer in Cork.

Before Strickland's enquiry began, Brigadier General Harold Whitla Higginson commander of the 17th Infantry Brigade in Victoria Barracks, held his own military enquiry, interviewing a number of soldiers based in the barracks. The main purpose of this enquiry seems to have been to clear the military of wrongdoing, which not surprisingly it did, pointing the finger of blame squarely at the Auxiliaries and RIC.

The Strickland Enquiry was held from 16 December in Victoria Barracks. On 13 December *The Cork Examiner* published the following announcement: 'All persons willing to give evidence in this case, and in a position to do so are requested to communicate with these headquarters as early as possible. Name of witness will not be published in press.' Witnesses who attended the enquiry would only be allowed into the enquiry one by one. Strickland barred members of the press, giving the reason that witnesses had been given a guarantee that their names could not be published and the evidence, if published, would reveal who they were. Moreover, no lawyers were allowed to be present, ensuring that any professional bodies or interested parties could not be represented.

Maurice Healy, a well-known Cork solicitor, had written to Strickland on 16 December, only to be informed that lawyers would not permitted to attend. Healy wrote again the next day and on 20 December, but a reply on 21 December stated 'that as the court of enquiry has now closed, your question does not arise'. This seemed to confirm the general belief that the military enquiry was a sham.

On 14 February 1921 Prime Minister Lloyd George said of Strickland's report: 'If it is published it is an unpleasant document. It says that there is evidence that the R.I.C. were seen firing the buildings, that there were numerous cases of looting by the troops, that the discipline of the troops was inadequate', to which Bonar Law replied, 'Strickland has since told me that with his present knowledge the report is not true to the facts. In any case it was not intended for publication.' But Winston Churchill observed with characteristic bluntness, 'On the whole, with the dangerous situation in Ireland, to publish would only complicate things and give ammunition to the enemy.'

As a result, this report was never published and the British government stuck to its guns, refusing to take responsibility for the events of 11 December until much later.

General Strickland, KBC, KBE, CMG, DSO, commander of the 6th Infantry Division in Victoria Barracks, who chaired the military enquiry into the burning of Cork. (Courtesy of Mercier Archive)

Bishop Cohalan (*left*), whose decree of excommunication caused consternation amongst the IRA. (Courtesy of Mercier Archive)

# BISHOP COHALAN'S DECREE

While the British government's reaction is perhaps not particularly surprising in the context of the time, the attempt to shift the ultimate blame for the burning onto the republican movement by one of Cork's own is much more so. At midday mass on Sunday 12 December in the North Cathedral, Bishop Daniel Cohalan, alarmed by the scale of the violence that had engulfed his diocese, condemned the arson but said that the burning of the city was a result of the 'murderous ambush at Dillon's Cross'. He vowed, in a speech that was printed in the following day's *Examiner*, that 'I will certainly issue a decree of excommunication against anyone who, after this notice, shall take part in an ambush or a kidnapping or attempted murder or arson.' Bishop Cohalan insisted 'that anyone who organised or took part in an ambush or in kidnapping or otherwise, shall be guilty of murder, or attempt at murder, and shall incur by the very fact the censure of excommunication'. The following week Cohalan issued a pastoral letter which was read at all masses across his Cork diocese, reaffirming this decree of excommunication. His condemnation was ill-received by his Catholic flock, who had two priests, Fr Michael Griffin in Galway city and Canon Thomas J. Magner near Dunmanway, killed by rampaging Auxiliaries in November and December 1920 respectively.

There was widespread resentment of the excommunication decree and many members of Cork Corporation openly criticised it. A meeting of the corporation was held on the afternoon of Monday 14 December at the municipal offices. As reported in *The Cork Examiner* of 15 December, Councillor J. J. Walsh condemned the bishop for his comments, which he claimed held the Irish people up as the 'evil-doers'. Walsh noted that while the people of Cork had been suffering, 'not a single word of protest was uttered by the bishop, and today, after the city has been decimated, he saw no better course than to add insult to injury'. Councillor Michael Ó Cuill, Alderman Tadhg Barry and Lord Mayor O'Callaghan all agreed with Walsh's sentiments.

Tom Barry was in the Mercy Hospital recovering from a heart condition when he learned of Bishop Cohalan's decree of excommunication. He was very aware of the grave impact such a decree would have on the morale of the West Cork Brigade, as the majority of these men were deeply religious. Barry's own reaction, however, was one of anger. In *Guerilla Days* he stated that if the IRA laid down their arms, as requested by the bishop, at least 200 Cork IRA men would be killed by the British forces within a week. Furthermore, he pointed out that Dr Cohalan had not even obtained a promise safeguarding IRA members or guaranteeing that no executions or murders would take place if the fight for independence stopped.

Liam Deasy recalled, in his memoir *Towards Ireland Free*, that on New Year's Day 1921 Barry and himself attended mass at Enniskeane, officiated by the parish priest Fr O'Connell. Fr O'Connell recognised Deasy and Barry, and invited them both to breakfast at the presbytery, a potentially perilous move considering that the Auxiliaries had murdered the neighbouring parish priest, Canon Magner, just two weeks before. Fr O'Connell made no secret of his disapproval of Dr Cohalan's pastoral letter, a feeling privately shared by many priests in the diocese.

An interesting postscript to the issue of Bishop Cohalan's actions took place on Christmas Eve when a number of armed IRA men, about thirty in number, wrecked the printing press of *The Cork Examiner* at Faulkner's Lane (now Opera Lane). Having cut the telephone wires so help could not be summoned, two men stood guard over the caretaker and the rest 'went quickly to the printing room and bombed the machine used in connection with the printing of the evening edition of the *Examiner* and the *Echo*'. An attempt was also made to destroy two other rotary printing machines located at

*Left:*

**Canon Thomas Magner, parish priest of Dunmanway, was murdered by Cadet Vernon Hart of K Company shortly after the company's arrival in County Cork. (Author's collection)**

Bowling Green Street, which also belonged to the *Examiner*. Fortunately the two bombs placed under them failed to explode or they would have been reduced to scrap metal. The paper's supposed crime against the Republic had been the publication, just days before, of Bishop Cohalan's pastoral letter condemning the violence of all sides of the War of Independence and reaffirming his threat of excommunication. The editor noted that if the attack on the printing presses had been successful, 120 people would have immediately become unemployed. Just the day previously the *Examiner* had carried an article appealing for the raising of funds to relieve distress in Cork, imploring employers not to add to the unemployment of the city but to retain every employee for whom it was possible to find any work.

Bishop Cohalan was the only Irish bishop to issue a decree of excommunication.

**A *Cork Examiner* printing press similar to one attacked by Republicans on Christmas Eve. (Courtesy of the *Irish Examiner*)**

Spectators look at the damage to their city. The American Commission stated that 'The actual losses represented by the fires on that night have been estimated at somewhere in the region of two and a half or three millions [pounds].' (Courtesy of Mercier Archive)

# COMPENSATION CLAIMS

Following the destruction in Cork, 602 claims for compensation were made. The amount of compensation paid to the owners of the destroyed premises dictated the quality and standard of the rebuilding in the affected area. Insurance proved to be a major stumbling block, as the vast majority of the premises concerned held insurance policies for riot and commotion, which only compensated for stock, not the buildings themselves. The British government was adamant that no compensation would be paid by it, ruling that it was the local authority's responsibility, so the only recourse to reimbursement for those affected was to lodge a claim on the rate-payers of the city, through the corporation.

The American Commission on Conditions in Ireland provided a detailed list of the amounts being claimed by businesses and landlords, which they believed would not be anything like the figures needed for reconstruction. However, their conception of what would be needed was probably higher than what was actually necessary. For instance, the first claim recorded as being lodged with the town clerk was by the corporation for City Hall and the Carnegie Free Library and its contents, and the claim was for £280,000. As City Hall was actually rebuilt for around £120,000, it seems that the money asked for would probably have been more than enough to cover the cost of rebuilding the two premises, as well as replacing the contents in the library.

According to the commission, the following are the amounts that were lodged with the town clerk, who was acting on behalf of the corporation:

| | |
|---|---|
| Corporation: City Hall and Carnegie Free Library, and contents | £280,000 |
| The Munster Arcade – Messrs Robertson, Ledlie & Ferguson, 27–30 Patrick Street, 99–102 Georges Street, and 3 Robert Street | £450,000 |

Cork Furniture Stores, 22 Merchant Street £8,406

William Roche, 15 Patrick Street and 21 Maylor Street £17,000

Messrs Roches Stores (London House) £112,000

T. Lyons & Co., 52–54 Patrick Street £120,000

Charles C. Harvey, premises Munster Arcade and 27–28 Patrick
  Street £31,158

Messrs Cash & Co., 18–21 Patrick Street and 24–25 Maylor Street £250,000

Saxone Shoe Co., 24 Patrick Street £30,000

Wm Egan & Sons Ltd £100,000

Lee Boot Manufacturing Co., 16 Patrick Street and 21 Maylor Street £19,000

Wm Cashman & Co. Ltd, 4 Cook Street £30,000

Annie Nolan, 18–21 Patrick Street (premises) £50,000

James Donovan for premises 52–54 Patrick Street (Grant & Co.) and
  51 Patrick Street (Samuel Haynes) £37,000

A. M. Walker, 30 Patrick Street (premises, Munster Arcade) £20,000

James Ryan, 26 Maylor Street and 21–22 Merchant Street £24,000

Ed Woods, 3 Cook Street £6,000

Richard Sunner, 31 Patrick Street £26,000

Messrs Forrest & Sons, Patrick Street, Cook Street and Elbow Lane £95,000

J. T. O'Regan, 25–26 Patrick Street £40,000

J. Tyler and Sons, 20 Winthrop Street £12,750

R. & J. McKechnie Ltd, 25 Patrick Street £21,000

Marcus Forester Harvey, 25–26 Patrick Street, 1–9 Robert Street and
  103–104 Georges Street £10,000

Simon Spiro, 9 Bridge Street and 3 Patrick's Quay £3,675

W. Roche and Lee Boot Manufacturing Co., 16 Patrick Street and 21
  Maylor Street £17,000

Lessees in leases of Lee Cinema, Winthrop Street £10,000

Mary Perry, 1–2 Winthrop Street £10,000

Rev. F. H. Sandys and others, 26 Patrick Street £9,000

T. F. Carroll, 13 Patrick Street and 103 Georges Street £11,000

When the corporation saw the size of the claims, they realised they would not have the funds to cover such amounts and so took the unusual step of ruling that the county council would have to pay 50 per cent of the awards.

The first insurance claim to be heard, in the presence of the Honorary Recorder of Cork, KC, and Lloyd's Insurance Company, was for The Munster Arcade, in which the proprietors, Messrs Robertson, Ledlie, Ferguson & Co. Ltd, made a claim for £450,000. A record of the hearing relating to this claim from the 'Report of the City Engineer Concerning the Conflagration in the City on 11th and 12th December 1920' is worth recording in full here, as it gives an interesting account of what the night was like for the employees who lived on the premises:

**According to Alfred Hutson, the only way such total devastation could have been caused to buildings like Sunner's, seen here, was if the fires were started deliberately and 'a considerable amount of petrol or some such inflammable was used'. (Courtesy of the National Library of Ireland)**

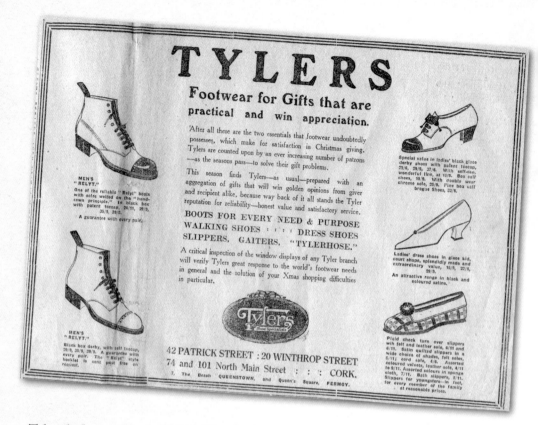

**Tylers had several branches of shoe shops in Cork. They claimed compensation for their Winthrop Street premises which was destroyed, although their premier shop in Patrick Street had luckily survived. (Author's collection)**

Messrs D. H. Connor, KC, and Mr George Daly (instructed by Mr J. J. Horgan solr) appeared for the applicants. There was also a claim by Captain Crosbie Charles Harvey, of Kyle, head landlord of the premises, and Mr F. Cotter (instructed by Messrs Stanton and Sons solrs) appeared for him.

Mr Patrick Barry gave evidence that he was employed as a dispatch clerk in the Munster Arcade and that he slept on the premises on the night of the fire. He locked up the domestic part of the store about 9.30 and there were then on the premises with him two apprentices and three women. After locking up the premises he was in a room when the housekeeper came down to him and said that there were places on fire.

He opened the shop for one of the watchmen and placed the other at the window overlooking Robert Street. He also put an apprentice on the window overlooking Elbow Lane and went to the front of the store himself with another apprentice named Collins. He then saw that Grant's was on fire, and he saw police and soldiers with a lorry outside the place. Shortly after an ambulance passed down Patrick Street. He saw police with rifles moving down Patrick Street, and he saw a tram on fire near Mangan's. He saw one policeman apparently carrying cans of petrol and he heard noise as if shutters were broken. Police were moving up and down, following a Crossley car in which were soldiers. The latter shouted 'Cheerio' to the police, and the police replied by shouting 'Cheerio'. He saw a bunch of police going down Maylor Street, and immediately after he heard an explosion near the domestic portion of Cash's in Maylor Street. He saw some girls and men coming out of Cash's. He then saw three police pass under him, and they started to break the glass at Burton's, after which he heard a shout, 'The Munster Arcade next.'

A crowd came underneath the stairs, the shutters were pulled apart, and the glass broken. The police then threw a bomb into the shop underneath where Patrick Barry was. He went back and got the rest of employees together. He then went to the window overlooking Elbow Lane, where he saw about ten or eleven police. He spoke to them and told them that there were women in the store. The answer was given by an officer who told him to put his hands up. Witness said that he had the keys of the place, and was ordered to come down and open the door. He did so, and all the time there were bombs exploding in the shop. They were then all marched out, covered with revolvers and placed against Wood's gate in Elbow Lane. While they were held there, an officer and a policeman went upstairs in the Arcade with petrol. They were there for some minutes, when witness saw gushes of flame coming from the dining hall.

While they were upstairs the other policemen started to put masks on their faces. After some time the witness's party were released, and they went towards Georges Street, but they were ordered back by police who fired a few rounds at them, but witness thought that the shots were fired in the air. They then endeavoured to go towards the Victoria Hotel, but they were ordered back by a party of police there. They then went around Marlboro Street, where all the windows were smashed.

Mrs Gaffney, a housekeeper at the Munster Arcade, answering questions by Mr Daly, gave generally corroborative evidence. When the last witness told the police that there were women in the place, she heard a reply 'Hold up your hands, the women are safe, whatever about you.' When the door was opened she saw police in the lane, and the officer had a muffler up to his eyes and carried a revolver. He went upstairs and carried two heavy-looking bags with him. When they were lined up in the lane, she asked an auxiliary officer to let her go back and put on some clothes, but was refused, the man saying, 'No Madam you didn't consider us, we will not consider you.'

Finbarr McAuliffe, an apprentice also corroborated the evidence. When he was told by Patrick Barry to go to the kitchen he heard five or six shots fired through the lock. About two minutes after, the officer and police went upstairs; they saw flames coming through the windows. When they were released, they saw parties whom they took to be fugitives like themselves leaving Robert Street, and they went in their direction. They found however, that they were police, and they fired a few shots at them. There were also uniformed men at the Victoria Hotel who turned them back.

At the sitting of the court on Friday the Recorder gave judgement in the claim of Messrs Robertson, Ledlie, Ferguson & Co., Ltd., for £450,000 for the malicious burning of the Munster Arcade on the 11–12 December. He said that in going through the items, as he had done with some care, he had found that the sums erred on the side of excess. He had gone through the various items with such care that he could, scrutinising them pretty minutely and he found it necessary to discount several of them. The entire amount of which evidence was given came to £260,927 11s 9d. He had made a deduction of £47,280 and would award compensation for £213,647.

Although the British had initially refused to take responsibility, as part of the negotiations for the Anglo-Irish Treaty of 1921 at the end of the Civil War it was agreed that a British compensation commission would set up. Lord Shaw of Dunfermline was chairman, James C. Dowdall was the Irish representative and C. J. Howell Thomas was the British representative. The payments awarded by this commission would be paid out by the British and would be instead of corporation payments. This of course served to delay what was already a slow process, as did wrangling over the amounts to be paid out. In an article in *The Cork Examiner* of 8 June 1922, it was suggested that reductions of between 40 and 70 per cent were to be awarded in line with Sir Hamar Greenwood's policy that Irish claims should be reduced by 50 per cent. This caused major consternation to the beleaguered businesses, as most probably the recorder's original awards would be reduced by a very considerable amount. On Thursday 1 June 1922 Egan's were awarded £34,608, which was substantially lower than the £54,394 promised by the recorder at the first hearings on compensation on 16 February but which was subsequently not paid as a result of the British acceptance of responsibility. However, the claim by Sunner's Chemist remained unchanged from the original Cork hearing, and Grant's were awarded £107,813.

Other claims included those made by Lyon's, who received £32,406 for stock and £22,238 for their premises. They had spent £5,380 on temporary premises leaving them with just £16,858 for reconstruction. William Roche claimed compensation for The London House, with a list of contents which included a unionist flag lost in the inferno. His manager, Pat Fitzgerald, believed that their case was treated more sensitively as it was thought the flag indicated unionist sympathies.

Further delays to payouts of compensation were caused by the Civil War of June 1922–May 1923, which meant progress on rebuilding was painfully slow. A *Cork Examiner* report of November 1923 noted that 'the condition of Patrick Street was a disgrace to the city. The principal thoroughfare was like a graveyard.' It was not until March 1924 that progress really began to be made as rebuilding began in earnest.

RUINS FROM EGANS TO CASH & CO'S.

*Opposite top:*

The ruins of Patrick Street from Egan's to Cash's. According to a Labour Party eyewitness, an Auxiliary told an ex-officer that 'as Cash's had been so badly looted they were going to set it on fire in order to cover up the loot'. (Author's collection)

*Opposite bottom:*

A man on the left peers through a window at the destroyed interior of City Hall while several boys pose outside. (Courtesy of Mercier Archive)

*Below:*

In an enquiry into the demolition of the Carnegie Free Library in 1924, the external walls of which appeared largely undamaged, the new lord mayor, Sean French, defended the decision: 'The Carnegie Library when viewed from the outside looked rather good and solid … [but] there was a grave doubt expressed by our advisers as to the possibility of it carrying a new floor. With the intense heat caused by the fire and the hosing of water to prevent it, the limestone in the building was ruined.' (Author's collection)

An aerial view of the city showing the many fine new buildings that were constructed on Patrick Street. In the background City Hall is still under construction. (Author's collection)

# REBUILDING CORK CITY

William Roche left the following account of the financial and security difficulties facing his business in the immediate aftermath of the fire, recorded in Healy's *The Story of Roches Stores*:

> Our difficulty now was to protect the salvaged goods from looters as, of course, there was only a minimum of police protection. That night we put a few men on the premises, that is, in some secondary premises which we had, but they told us the following morning that they had been overpowered during the night and that looters took a quantity of goods. A few of us traders went to the military for protection against these looters; the officer promised most kindly to do what he could in the circumstances and it must have been effectual as we had no more trouble after that.
>
> We were now up against it once more. Firstly I owed the [Hibernian] bank a very large sum and, of course, now my visible assets were very little. Added to this, on 1st of December 1920, we had bought additional premises for a good sum; these premises, which we had not got possession of, were also burned down and I was legally responsible and bound in two months' time to pay for them. I asked the sellers, who are perhaps the biggest business people in Cork, as I was in such a hole, would they release me and call the deal off. No, they would not do it.

Fortunately for Roche, the bank agreed to stand by him if he reduced his overdraft. Roche also had a plan for getting back into business quickly:

> We still had some old premises in Merchant Street. No electric light, no gas, as all the mains were destroyed. Battered roofs and in a rotten state of repair. We got in twenty-

five or thirty of our staff at once, who worked at all hours and in this confusion amid falling walls we started a sale.

Pat Fitzgerald takes up the story:

For a month previous to the fire we had taken the precaution of putting into position each night a corrugated iron partition across the narrow neck that divided the two large squares forming the warehouse, and to the back square we removed each night a large portion of valuable goods. We were rewarded for our efforts when the fire did come, a fair quantity of goods behind this barrier being saved. It was this stock which enabled us to restart in the Merchant Street premises a few days after the burnings. We were the first of the affected firms to get going and had a large Calico Sign erected on the Patrick Street ruins announcing 'Salvage Sale at Roche's Stores'.

Even while the premises were burning on Sunday morning, December 12th, Mr Roche was formulating plans for the carrying on of the business at Merchant Street premises. The plans were dependent on Merchant Street escaping the fire, which it mainly did through an employee of Lambkin's who travelled astride his firm's roof to a spot which had caught fire and with a wet bag and a watering can put out the flame before it had got a hold on the building which adjoined our premises (No. 22). The plans then put forward were those adopted and put into use a few days later when Lloyd's inspector had examined the saved goods.

Roche notes that on the opening of the Merchant Street premises:

In a round week we sold double as much as we would have sold in our main premises. It was rough work. Three or four scuffles a day with robbers was in the routine. When we caught these pilferers which were mostly men, we took the goods from them, took the law into our hands, gave them a good hiding and pitched them into the street.

One incident which, I am thankful to say, did not leave tragedy behind, was the sudden collapse of a wall at the entrance to the side street which led to our premises. Generally there were a great number of people passing, coming down to our sale, but it suddenly fell when the street was clear. This blocked the direct access to our premises

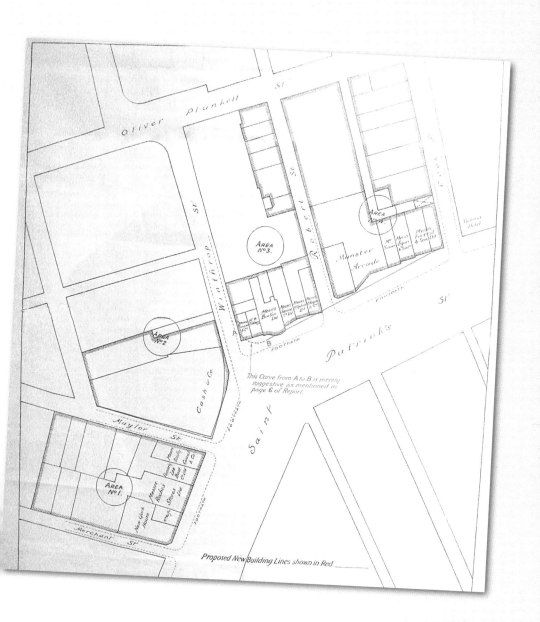

**A map showing the proposed new rebuilding lines by the reconstruction committee. (Author's collection)**

and was closed forthwith for all traffic. We then stationed several men at points along a new route, who through the windings of an obscure alley shouted out and pointed the way to Roches Stores. Amid all this confusion, the money poured into the Bank …

For six months or more we worked in the old stores in Merchant Street, where we had this sale; early in the summer following the fire we got into temporary wooden premises, erected on the site of the burned building.

According to Pat Fitzgerald:

These were undoubtedly the best of the temporary premises erected at the time and were put up in record time by Mr. Goove, the builder, in just one month. The sale had run its course and figures dropped to zero; the records of the time will show that from the first days trading in Patrick Street our sales jumped to about double and kept on increasing which shows the value of a good location for retail trade.

But the company still faced financial problems, as noted by Roche:

We, of course, were now running at a considerable loss in trading with no reserves, it was evident that this could not go on for long. The ordinary insurance which we had on stock and premises was useless; we had taken out a policy for riot and civil commotion on stock only, not on buildings.

It was Pat Fitzgerald's job to help prove the claim for compensation by listing the fitting and fixtures destroyed. He noted that:

One of the items listed was a flag, and at a later stage when Mr. Gifford, the British Treasury Agent, was finally disposing of the case this small item was questioned. On our stating that the flag was a Union Jack, Mr. Gifford declared the amount would certainly be allowed to stand. To say the least, I think it had some influence on the case. As a matter of fact, we had never flown the flag having inherited it from the London House, among such various items.

As rebuilding commenced on Egan's, their temporary premises was removed and they relocated their business to 45 MacCurtain Street. They received £34,608 in compensation from the Shaw Commission, almost £20,000 lower than the initial Cork Corporation award. (Author's collection)

Even with the claim made and approved, Roche noted that:

> The payment of this amount [of compensation] was much delayed because of the fixing of the Liability for the destruction; eventually we got most of the money 'on loan' from the underwriters, and this sum paid into the Bank relieved the financial pressure which was then on us. Our claim was then made for compensation to the public authorities. We got a substantial decree, but the local authorities had neither the funds nor the desire to pay these claims. Eventually, after the inevitable delays, our claim was settled by the British government.

Temporary structures became the order of the day while the business of gaining compensation and planning the new buildings was carried out. However, the whole process of rebuilding took longer than might have been expected.

On 18 May 1921 the minute book of the Cork Corporation records that one member from each electoral area was to be appointed to supervise the work of reconstruction in the city. The minute book also recorded various suggestions to change the landscape of the city. By the summer this reconstruction committee had met six times and their main concern seemed to be the lines of rebuilding and that no ill-designed premises would be constructed on the existing sites.

The suggested changes to the layout of the city centre would seriously complicate the process of rebuilding, as many of the premises owners objected to these proposed changes. For example, the suggestion to remove Robert Street was opposed by O'Regan's hosiers, who were located on the corner of Robert Street and Patrick Street. They were afraid that the scheme would affect their prominent position in Patrick Street. In fact, unsurprisingly the majority of property owners on Robert Street were opposed to this idea and the city solicitor advised that the street could not be closed without the consent of all the owners. Another suggestion,

**Chillingworth & Levie's drawing of Cook Street was prepared for the firm of Forrest's and showed the projected buildings of 34 Patrick Street and Nos 1, 2 & 3 Cook Street. (Courtesy of Cork City & County Archives)**

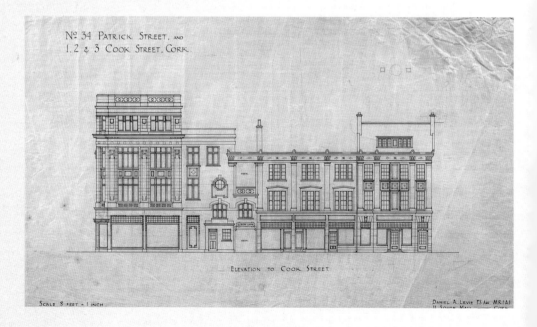

to rearrange the sites of many of the destroyed premises with a view to widening Winthrop Street, meant the reduction of the frontage of businesses on the street. A proposal to round off the corner of Patrick Street onto Cook Street was opposed by Messrs Forrest whose business was located there. Their architects, Chillingworth & Levie, sent a letter to the corporation on their behalf. Meanwhile Miss Woulfe and J. O'Sullivan were seeking compensation for proposed loss of ground on Patrick Street.

Although there appears to have been some effort made to get the rebuilding process moving, as Messrs Scully and O'Connell's application for a permit to build a semi-permanent structure was rejected on 4 August because it would be an impediment to permanent rebuilding, little progress was made on the actual reconstruction of the city in 1921. The only glimpse of progress was when O'Regan's, at 26 Patrick Street, became the first firm to open its new premises for business, on Saturday 26 November 1921, but this would be the only new building opened that year.

The first half of 1922 saw little progress. In March Messrs O'Flynn and O'Connell's plans for the new building for the Saxone Shoe Co. were rejected by the reconstruction committee. Then, when the Civil War erupted in June, all rebuilding plans were put on hold, while the hearing for the awards by the compensation commission could not proceed during a time of war. This situation was exacerbated when the Irish Labour movement organised a nationwide strike agitating for a peaceful resolution to the war. After republican forces evacuated Cork city in August, some progress was made in September when a motion was passed to close all temporary structures and erect permanent ones in their place. However, the temporary structures had to remain in place while their replacements were constructed.

Progress was also made on the issue of realignment of the streetscape. When the corporation had made it clear that it wished to acquire the Misses Thompson's premises on the corner of Winthrop Street so the widening of that street could go ahead, the owners were initially not prepared to negotiate a private sale. Despite this, by 20 December 1922 the corporation had somehow purchased the property. Cash's conceded the widening of Maylor Street by three feet and of Caroline Street, where they were planning to take over the premises of John Daly, by ten inches. Those who agreed to changes in building lines which meant a decrease in the size of their original premises were entitled to compensation. For example, Burton's sought a large sum due to plans to change their frontage. Cudmore's, who were next door to Burton's, refused to grant any portion of their site to their neighbour.

Although some progress was being made, the process of reconstruction was still moving incredibly slowly. On 13 January 1923 a meeting of the corporation heard that 6,000 people were still unemployed as a result of the burning two years previously. But this issue did not seem to have any impact on Burton's grandiose plans for their new building, which involved the use of Sicilian marble fascias and Norwegian granite. The Trade Workers Council were insisting that Irish workers and materials be used and stated that they would prevent the importation of any stone. Burton's problems were exacerbated when, on 2 March, Cork Corporation urged the Minister for Finance not to pay a 5 per cent allowance on the awards made by the Shaw Commission unless Burton's proceeded with rebuilding. It seemed a stalemate had been reached – Burton's could not move forward without money or workers, but to get these they would have to change their plans, which they were clearly not willing to do.

Other issues such as the paying of rates came into play and a deputation of owners met with the corporation on 3 June 1923 seeking to have any rateable valuation held at pre-burning levels to aid recovery, an issue that took nearly two years to resolve. Despite this, a number of companies wrote to the corporation in that year stating that plans and drawings were being commissioned and that work on rebuilding would commence shortly. However, by December Grant's had just awarded their rebuilding contract to John Delaney & Co., which meant that the rebuilding would not begin until January 1924 at the earliest. Cudmore's were still awaiting estimates for work, while Cash's were busy negotiating the purchase of John Daly's premises. The plans for Tylers had been submitted for consideration but had not yet been approved, and Burton's were blaming the local trades for lack of progress on their rebuilding efforts.

By 1924 the first signs of major reconstruction were finally visible. The front wall of the American Shoe Co. was almost at full height and stonemasons were

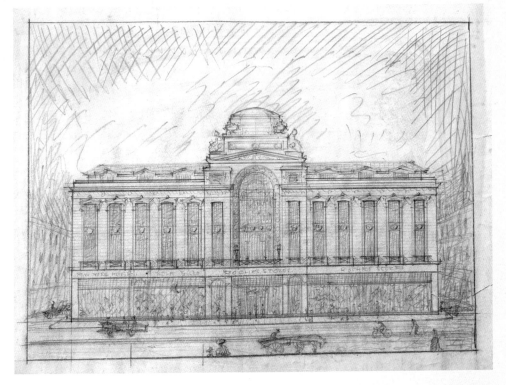

**Chillingworth & Levie's original drawing for the front of the new Roches Stores building. Government buildings were on the upper floors with a separate entrance on Maylor Street. (Courtesy of Cork City & County Archives)**

working on Egan's. Cudmore's had steel girders to first-floor level, while Grant's had extended their site by acquiring the site of what had been Haynes & Son jewellers. Significant street realignment had taken place.

Irish labour and material were ongoing concerns for the rebuilding programme with different agendas on the table. The issue of the heating of buildings was brought up at a corporation meeting by Councillor McCarthy and it was stated that a Cork contractor could undertake this work. The corporation had invited the Macroom Engineering Co. and the Cork firm of Pulvertaft to quote for the brass fittings for Cudmore's, while Youghal brick was to be used by the American Shoe Co. The Burton materials dispute was still not resolved, and the Cork Development Association became involved, advocating the use of Irish marble and limestone. The

**After its rebuilding Roches Stores established a reputation for great value. The annual sale became known to Corkonians as the 'real' sale. (Author's collection)**

association outlined seven advantages to using Irish materials, including a longer lifespan. Grant's was also having material issues – they wanted to use metal window frames instead of timber on their premises. The trades objected to the work being allocated abroad and insisted on timber, which was eventually agreed to by the architect, Mr McMullen.

There were other impediments to some of the reconstruction. Mrs Murphy's temporary structure in Winthrop Street was not located in its proper position, which was stopping progress being made on adjoining buildings. Other businesses felt that their plans were not being given proper consideration for approval by the corporation. On 31 October, by ministerial order, this body was officially dissolved and, shortly afterwards, Philip Monahan was appointed local authority manager of the city.

In 1925 the rateable valuation of the premises was finally resolved, the terms being that the valuation of 1920 would be maintained until 1930. The proviso was that the owners concerned undertake to start rebuilding work immediately and that such an undertaking was faithfully complied with. By 24 October Egan's had been completed and was open for business. Grant & Co. was finished by 10 December. But two major projects had still not even started building – Cash's and Roches Stores.

William Roche of Roches Stores was taking a very resolute stance and was not about to be dictated to with regard to his rebuilding operation. First, he wanted to acquire the premises adjoining The London House: those of Scully, O'Connell & Co., the Lee Boot Company and Mrs Wolfe's, which were to be amalgamated into his new vision of a department store. Pat Fitzgerald, his manager said: 'Mr. Roche, for very good reasons, was slow to begin operations on the new building. Other property owners were also, for their own reasons, slow in starting. Pressure and intimidation was being brought to bear [presumably by the corporation] for the purpose of having the work begun. Mr. Roche, however, point blank defied the intimidators and we heard no more of the urgent need for starting the work, and began when it suited ourselves.'

William Roche also adopted a bellicose attitude to the demand by the trade's associations to use local labour and materials, and one would wonder how he got away with this. Was it because there was now enough work in the city to satisfy the labour movement and that they were working flat out just to complete the existing projects?

It took six years from the time of the burnings before the new building was completed at the enormous cost of £26,474 16s 10d, although Cash's rebuilding cost of £74,200 was the largest amount spent on any of the reconstructed buildings. Roche eventually contracted Cork architects Chillingworth & Levie, whilst the architect Henry Hill was awarded the Cash's contract and the builder was the Cork firm Sisk & Son. William Roche seems to have had a fairly low opinion of the building trade: 'The couple of years during which the building was being erected were very anxious years for us. We had had some experience of builders, architects, quantity surveyors, etc., and while I suppose they are as much inclined as any others in this very immoral country to give value for money, we were quite aware that unless we saw to things ourselves, we ran a good chance of being let down.'

Seeing to things themselves led to some disagreement between client and architect. Fitzgerald recorded that 'Mr Roche insisted on the present large fascia letters, though the architects fought for something "neat and dignified". The letters proved their worth as the premises today are known as Roches Stores and not "Government Offices" – a contingency which we feared since the upper portion of the building had been leased to them.'

It appears that Roche was given a free hand unlike some of his business peers, as local labour and materials were not used exclusively in his rebuilding campaign. Unlike the Grant's situation, many of the window frames in the new Roches stores were made by the Manchester firm of Humphrey Jackson & Amber Ltd, and the glass countertops were made of Flemish not Irish glass. The lavatories were manufactured by the unlikely sounding Northern Art Pavement Co. Ltd of Manchester and London.

The new Roches Stores finally opened its doors to the Cork public in January 1927, although building work would not be completed until some time later.

*Above:*

This image of the new Roches Stores building shows it still under construction, but open for business on the ground floor. (Courtesy of the *Irish Examiner*)

*Right:*

Cash's curved Little Island limestone façade was designed by Henry H. Hill and the building was completed at the enormous cost of £74,200. (Courtesy of the *Irish Examiner*)

Just three years later, the trams were gone. Although the tram poles remained on the street until the 1960s, for some reason they have been deliberately erased from this 1920s postcard image. It appears that the Tylers premises were not yet completed as hoarding at the front is still evident. (Author's collection)

Tram poles are still evident in this street scene, although the trams themselves had disappeared from the streetscape in 1931, having lasted for a period of thirty-three years. (Author's collection)

PATRICK

CORK.

The long-established firms of The Munster Arcade and Egan (next to Tylers) continued their tradition of trading in Patrick Street in their new enhanced premises. (Author's collection)

St. Patrick Street, Cork. 661.

The new public Cork City Library at 57–58 Grand Parade, the spiritual successor of the Carnegie, was built on the site of former warehouses and officially opened in September 1930. (Courtesy of Cork City Library)

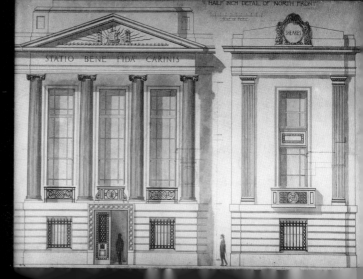

A detail of a speculative architectural design for the rebuilding of the City Hall by the architects O'Flynn and O'Connor. (Courtesy of Cork Public Museum)

## CITY HALL

One of the last buildings in the city to be reconstructed was City Hall. The remains of both the old City Hall and the Carnegie Free Library had been demolished at a cost of £2,359. However, reservations were later expressed about this decision and, at a local government enquiry into administration by Cork Corporation in 1925, local builder Thomas Kelleher stated that if they had been his buildings he would not have taken them down, particularly the Carnegie Free Library, which he believed could have been reconstructed at very little expense as the main walls were practically intact. Sir Stanley Harrington of the Cork Progressive Association said that in his opinion a large portion of the City Hall might have been made quite serviceable. The lord mayor at that time was Sean French, who dismissed both men's opinions and vigorously defended the corporation's decision to demolish the buildings.

Following the destruction of the original building no temporary premises were constructed for the use of Cork Corporation staff, and they appear to have been based in the courthouse until 1924. Following the dissolution of the corporation in October 1924, purportedly because of its excessive rates, inefficiency and wasting of funds, although in reality this was probably part of a move by the Irish government to get rid of corporations nationwide that were dominated by anti-Treaty members, Philip Monahan was appointed as the city's first local authority manager. He took up his appointment on 11 November 1924.

One of Monahan's first actions was to close the City Museum at Fitzgerald's Park so that it could be used as civic offices. In a letter to *The Cork Examiner,* published on 10 December 1924, he stated that the temporary accommodation at Fitzgerald's Park was satisfactory and that it would be more appropriate to spend the £58,000 at his disposal following the compensation award for City Hall on houses for the working classes, rather than on a luxury municipal building. True to his word the first of many housing schemes of fifty houses in Fair Hill was completed in 1927.

The initial six bids to rebuild City Hall were well over the allocated amount:

# CORK BURNING

1. Maguire and Short, Mulgrave Road, Cork:     £61,033 7s 10d

2. Alexander Hall and Company, Dublin:     £61,507

3. John Sisk & Son Builders, Cork:     £65,980

4. Jeremiah Murphy, North Abbey Street, Cork:     £66,706

5. Meagher & Hayes, Cork:     £70,962 15s 6d

6. John Hearne & Son, Waterford:     £72,453

Before he made the decision to allocate the funds elsewhere, Monahan had ordered that the tenders be modified to reduce costs to within the budget. Yet when the building was finally rebuilt in the 1930s, it actually cost close to double the original amount allocated. The Dublin architects firm of Jones & Kelly was awarded the design contract and the Cork building firm John Sisk & Son built the new City Hall, with Cork stone being used for the majority of the project. The foundation stone was laid in 1932 and on 23 April 1935 the first meeting in the new building of Cork Corporation, which had been reinstituted in 1929, took place. The fully completed City Hall was officially opened by Éamon de Valera in 1936.

**While the colonnaded doorway was more ornate than the building it replaced, the new city hall, with its central clock tower, would have been fairly familiar to Cork's citizens. (Author's collection)**

The City Hall, Cork.

When the first meeting of Cork Corporation took place in the new building on 23 April 1935, admission to the public galleries was by ticket only. (Author's collection)

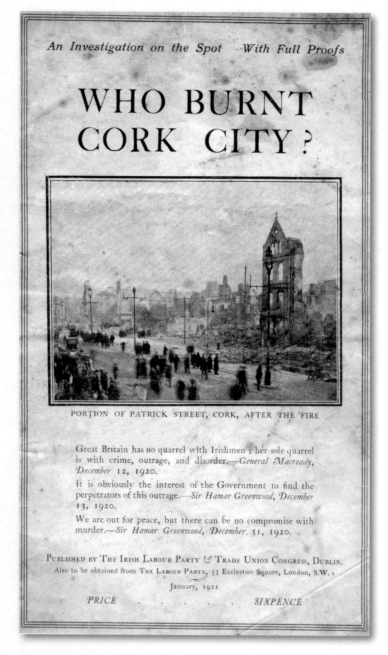

*An Investigation on the Spot    With Full Proofs*

# WHO BURNT CORK CITY?

PORTION OF PATRICK STREET, CORK, AFTER THE FIRE

Great Britain has no quarrel with Irishmen ; her sole quarrel is with crime, outrage, and disorder.—*General Macready, December* 12, 1920.

It is obviously the interest of the Government to find the perpetrators of this outrage.—*Sir Hamar Greenwood, December* 13, 1920.

We are out for peace, but there can be no compromise with murder.—*Sir Hamar Greenwood, December* 31, 1920.

PUBLISHED BY THE IRISH LABOUR PARTY & TRADE UNION CONGRESS, DUBLIN. Also to be obtained from THE LABOUR PARTY, 33 Eccleston Square, London, S.W. 1

January, 1921

*PRICE* . . . . *SIXPENCE*

**The front page of the published version of the Irish Labour Party's report on the burning of Cork, published in 1921. (Author's collection)**

# EPILOGUE

On 14 December 1920 K Company of the Auxiliaries, still under the command of Colonel Latimer, were moved to Dunmanway in West Cork, where their orgy of looting, terror and murder would continue. The rapidity of this move clearly shows that the British authorities knew that K Company bore a great deal of the responsibility for the burning of Cork. Of course, a government statement simply claimed that the move was prearranged.

Just a day later, on 15 December, two lorry-loads of Auxiliaries were travelling from Dunmanway to Cork for the funeral of Spencer Chapman, their comrade who was mortally wounded at Dillon's Cross. About a mile from the town the Auxiliaries passed a broken-down car and Vernon Hart, who was in command of one of the lorries, called on it to halt. He dismounted, and proceeded to kill Timothy Crowley, a farmer's son aged twenty-four, and Canon Thomas Magner, the seventy-three-year-old parish priest of Dunmanway, both of whom had stopped to help the driver of the car, Mr P. Brady. Brady, a local magistrate, escaped by fleeing across nearby fields. Hart was quickly arrested and court-martialled.

At his trial, it was revealed that he had been a particular friend of Chapman and had been drinking heavily since his death. The British cabinet directed that Hart should be examined by at least two medical experts, who testified that he was insane at the time of the murders. The court martial then concluded that he was guilty of the offences with which he was charged, but was insane at the time of their commission. Although Hamar Greenwood announced to the House of Commons that Hart would be detained at His Majesty's pleasure, he was only briefly held at Broadmoor Criminal Lunatic Asylum before being released the following year.

An Auxiliary, whose letter was quoted as an 'eyewitness statement' in the Irish

Labour Party report, said that on 16 December General H. W. Higginson arrived in Dunmanway to give them 'a straight talk' about 'discipline, &c.' However, 'I am afraid we struck terror into him for the "straight talk" never materialised.' Clearly Higginson's visit had little or no effect, as just days later, on 20 December, Auxiliary Samuel Baster forced a shopkeeper to issue him with a cheque for £150 during an unauthorised raid and was forced to resign his position.

On 15 February 1921 General Tudor told a cabinet meeting in London that there were about fifty men of K Company in Cork on the evening of the burning, and that he believed:

[T]here were seven or more men unfit to be in the service, and about 20 others ought to be got away from bad influences. The seven had not been dismissed, but they had been "run in" for other charges at Dunmanway. Four of them were accused of robbing a Bank. The K Company, to which all these men belonged, was being re-organised by getting rid of these men. It had not been possible to identify any one particular person as guilty of the Cork burnings. He had himself interrogated the Company … the burnings took place at 9.30 and the Colonel [Latimer] had taken charge of his men at 10 o'clock. Latimer denied that his men were implicated in the burning. They were, on the contrary, doing their utmost to put out the fires. He was with his men all night … The accommodation was of a very temporary character in Cork. Servants were living with the Cadets. Latimer could not get quarters for himself for an Office so the Deputy Constable allowed him to work at the Police Barracks and he lived in an hotel close by. He was there when the lorries came to him to report for orders. The bombing started at 300 yards off and he went and paraded his men.

Brigadier General Crozier, the man who formed K Company, seems to have become disillusioned with the crimes of the Auxiliaries in Ireland. In February 1921 he dismissed twenty-one Auxiliaries under his command after raids on Trim and Drumcondra left two young men dead. When Tudor, his superior, ordered the men reinstated, Crozier resigned in protest. Following his resignation, he published his case in the *London Daily News* and in his chronicle of events during his period of service he dealt with the burning of Cork:

A Colonel commanding a company of Auxiliaries at the time of the burning of Cork was suspended. When the company kicked up rough, all of those who were at Cork during the fires were sent to Dublin to be dealt with. What happened? They demanded the reinstatement of the Colonel or else they would state (1) Who burnt Cork; (2) The names of the men implicated; (3) The name of the man who pumped petrol on the City Hall and fired the Verey lights (flare gun) on to the roof. The result the Colonel was promoted [*sic*].

Crozier's airing of the Auxiliary Division's dirty laundry in public made it impossible for him to find further official employment. He unsuccessfully ran in the 1923 general election for the Labour Party for the Portsmouth Central seat. He then turned to writing and lecturing, but unpaid bills and dishonoured cheques were to dog him for the rest of his life. His books were controversial for their claims but were of doubtful factual accuracy. He was largely discredited and considered a nuisance by his contemporaries.

In *The Freeman's Journal* of 17 March 1921 it was reported that the chief secretary, in reply to questions in the House of Commons concerning the burning of Cork city, was asked if any of the Auxiliary Division or K Company had been punished, dismissed or suspended for acts committed during that night. Greenwood replied:

After the fullest investigation it has been found impossible to bring home to any individual member of this company any act in connection with the burnings in Cork for which he could be prosecuted, but seven who were strongly suspected of having been engaged in acts of indiscipline in regard to which, however, there was no proof, were put on trial for other offences of which there was evidence. Four were convicted of assault and of being engaged in an unlawful raid. Fines of £30 were imposed in three of the cases and a fine of £15 in the fourth. The services of the remaining three were dispensed with on the grounds of their general unsuitability as members of the force.

On 31 March 1921 the main instigators of the burning, K Company, were finally disbanded. So ended the sordid aftermath to the destruction of the centre of Cork city, which was filled with the British government's denials, fabricated evidence, lies and the blaming of Cork citizens for burning their own city. Despite several investigations, nobody was ever held to account for one of the single greatest acts of arson, vandalism, looting and murder committed by an occupying force whose duty was to protect life and property.

There was one final footnote to the events of 11–12 December. According to the records of another parliamentary debate on 2 June 1921, Lieutenant Commander Kenworthy asked the chief secretary if Colonel Latimer, who had commanded the Auxiliaries in Cork at the time of the burning, was still suspended from duty; if he had been tried, and, if so, with what result; and whether he was still employed in any way in Ireland, and, if so, in what capacity? Greenwood replied, 'The answer to the first two parts of the question is in the negative. As regards the last part, Colonel Latimer is at present doing duty with the Auxiliary Division as a temporary cadet.' Despite this, by 23 August 1921 Latimer's career had come to an ignominious end as he was suspended and struck off as a deserter.

# APPENDIX 1

# THE HIGGINSON ENQUIRY

On 13 December 1920 a military court of enquiry ordered by Brigadier General Higginson, commander of the Cork garrison, started to take evidence from his own men about what had happened on the night of 11–12 December. It was chaired by Major L. C. Morley of the 2nd Hampshire Regiment, and Major C. S. Reid and Captain F. A. Atchison were the other members of the enquiry panel. The evidence collected by this enquiry is summarised on The Auxiliary Division of the Royal Irish Constabulary website, and gives a clear sense that the military felt that the Auxiliaries were the main offenders of the evening.

The first witness, a lieutenant of the South Staffordshire Regiment, was in command of a patrol from 3 a.m. that night. Before going on patrol he saw a crowd of Auxiliaries and soldiers inside the barracks. He heard one of the Auxiliaries say, '"We are going out to burn the place down" or words to that effect.' Shortly afterwards an Auxiliary approached him and said, 'Are you coming with us, there is a good crowd in this platoon?' He sent the soldiers away.

Later, when on patrol, the lieutenant reported seeing two Auxiliaries firing revolvers at buildings, but he could not catch them. He also 'saw a few Auxiliary Police from time to time who did not appear to be under control. I saw one under the influence of drink.' The lieutenant also claimed he saw firemen and civilians who were drunk.

The second witness was a captain in charge of a curfew patrol of the 2nd Hampshire Regiment. He was on duty in the city centre from 10 p.m. 'At about 23.00 I went along the Grand Parade. I heard noises as if shutters were being pulled down and saw several parties of Auxiliary Police in front of shops. I came upon one Auxiliary policeman standing in front of a jewellery shop. The shutters had been pulled down. I asked him what he was doing and he replied that he was about to break the glass in order to set fire to the shop. When I spoke to him I was by myself. As there were several of his companions close at hand I could not take any action except search him and warn him, and [I] ordered him back to Barracks. At about the same time and near the same place I met a party of Auxiliary Police about 30 strong. I stopped them and told them that if they attempted to make any trouble in the town, my men would fire. Until the incident outside the jewellers shop I had no reason but to suppose that Auxiliary Police were in Cork City on duty … I stopped two Auxiliary policemen … who were carrying silver-mounted dressing cases and furs. I took possession of them and brought them back to the Bridewell. I could not take any other action as I had no troops with me and there was a large party of Auxiliaries close at hand … the parties of Auxiliary police, with the exception of a few individuals, appeared to be more or less under control …' The captain also claimed that the chief fire officer, several firemen, many civilians and even two of his own men were drunk.

The third witness was a lieutenant of the 2nd Hampshire Regiment, also on curfew patrol. At 10.15 p.m. he passed a party of Auxiliary police on Patrick Street marching under control and in military formation. At about 11 p.m. he saw a crowd of about thirty police and Auxiliaries opposite Mangan's jewellery shop. 'The shop had been forced open and I saw several Auxiliary Police coming out of it. Several members of the crowd were carrying suitcases. I did not see any silver articles or jewellery … I also noticed two Auxiliary Police who were keeping order among the civilians who were standing in the neighbourhood of fires … At about 05.00 when I was returning to Barracks with the Curfew Party I noticed an Auxiliary Policeman stop a civilian who was carrying loot. This policeman made the civilian hand over the loot and threw it back into the shop and ordered the civilian to clear off.'

The fourth witness was a lieutenant with the South Staffordshire curfew party. While on St Patrick's Bridge shortly after midnight, he noticed 'a party of Auxiliary police coming from Patrick St., they were not under any control. I noticed that they were carrying dressing cases and bundles.' He also claimed that he had seen drunk firemen.

The fifth witness, a second lieutenant in the 2nd Hampshire Regiment, seems to have seen the same Auxiliaries. He reported that while on curfew duty, 'Shortly after 22.00 I was passing Grant's shop which was on fire. I noticed an Auxiliary policeman come out of Grant's shop. He cheered us as we passed on a lorry … shortly after midnight as I passed Cash's shop, I noticed a crowd of Auxiliaries outside it. The shop had just been set on fire, and some Auxiliary police were heaping empty boxes on the flames. At the same time I heard one Auxiliary policeman say, "I only used half a tin of petrol". I asked if anyone was in charge and one replied that he was. I ordered him to march his party away and he did so. A party numbering about 20 did not go away with him. They appeared not to be under control. … While I was in Mangan's shop, a party of Auxiliaries passed me on their way to Patrick Bridge. They were not under any control and were carrying bundles and cases. While I was in Mangan's shop searching it, one of the sentries I had posted reported to me that one or two members of the Auxiliary Police had attempted to force him and enter the shop.'

The sixth witness, a Royal Engineers lieutenant who was in charge of the mobile searchlight stated, 'About 22.30 I was in the Court House in Workington [sic; Washington] Street, when I saw four Auxiliary Police cross the road, and a few minutes later I noticed a fire burning behind the Court House. I went to the scene of the fire and I noticed that a bicycle shop had been broken into and a pile of bicycles [was] burning in the middle of the road. There was no one in sight. At about 23.30 I noticed two Auxiliary police on the Grand Parade carrying bundles and at 01.00 I saw a drunken Auxiliary police outside the GPO.'

The seventh witness was a lieutenant on curfew duty with the South Staffordshire Regiment. Shortly after 10 p.m. he 'noticed a fire which had recently been started in Grant's shop. An Auxiliary policeman came out through an opening in the shop front. He waved his rifle at us and cheered and immediately afterwards I heard two shots go off. At about 02.00 I was in Patrick St. and I saw a party of Auxiliary police attempting to break into a shop with rifle butts. I took measures to send them away.'

The eighth witness was a corporal in the same regiment. He recalled that, 'At about 04.00 I was in charge of a patrol. When I was in Patrick Street I met a party of 4 Auxiliary police. One of them offered me some whiskey. I refused. He brandished his revolver and said to his companions, "Shall I loose off one or two here?" One of his companions replied, "No we have loosed off enough in the back streets. There is an officer down the road and we shall get into trouble if we do." Afterwards I was on duty near the GPO and I heard an Auxiliary policeman using filthy language to a woman.'

The ninth witness was a company sergeant major in the Military Foot Police. At 10.30 p.m., while checking on his own patrols, he came across a box of bombs left sitting by some Auxiliaries, who came to get them while he was still there. He also noted that at 9 p.m. he was outside the Empress Place RIC Barracks when about fifteen Auxiliaries stopped outside and shouted to some RIC recruits, 'Come on down we are going to send the place up tonight', or words to that effect. He noted that some of the Auxiliaries were under the influence of drink and at least one was wearing civilian clothes.

The tenth witness, a sergeant also in the Military Foot Police, stated that at 9.15 p.m. he 'saw a party of Auxiliary police advancing up King St. in marching order from the direction of Summer's Hill [sic]. They were shouting and discharging firearms at the same time. One of them came up to me and discharged two shots at me, but missed me and broke a plate glass window behind me. I said to him, "Don't you recognise a soldier?" He replied, "How the hell do I know who you are, nor do I care."' The sergeant gathered together the women living in the street, but when he had done so one of the Auxiliaries said to him, '"What the hell are you doing now?" I replied, "I was trying to protect these females from this wild conduct." He replied, "Take them to Bloody Hell, I shall shoot them as well as you." I got the women away safely.'

The eleventh witness, another sergeant in the Military Foot Police, saw a crowd of Auxiliaries near the butcher's in Ballyhooly Road discharging firearms at 7.30 p.m. Six Auxiliaries then passed his house and fired a shot at him. Around 10.30 p.m. two men in civilian clothes set fire to number 32, but later returned with a group of Auxiliaries to extinguish the fire.

The twelfth witness was a lance corporal in the 2nd Hampshire Regiment and was in charge of one of the curfew patrols. Shortly after midnight he was at Cash's. 'Inside the shop I saw several Auxiliary police, they were looting the shop and at the same time they were feeding the flames by throwing card boxes onto them. I ordered them out. One of them came up to me jokingly and said that they were trying to put the fire out. They refused to obey my orders ... at about this time an officer of the Auxiliary Police came up and said, "Fall in No. 1 Company of the Auxiliary Police." All the Auxiliaries fell in and marched off and took their loot with them in the direction of the GPO.' The lance corporal also said that he saw RIC and civilians looting and 'under the influence of drink'.

The thirteenth witness was a sergeant in the same regiment. He was in command of the guard at the main gate of Victoria Barracks. At 8.30 p.m. 'a party of Auxiliaries marched out of the barracks in the direction of Dillon's Cross, and that at 22.45 the same group returned, some under the influence of drink, and carrying dressing cases, overcoats, blankets and ladies' underwear. From this time onwards until about 01.45 there were continually parties of Auxiliaries passing into the barracks and nearly everyone was carrying something. At about 01.45 I received orders to stop any of the parties of Auxiliaries coming into the barracks.'

The evidence given by the next few witnesses was all along similar lines to that of earlier witnesses. A lieutenant in the Royal Field Artillery who was on duty in the city centre at about 4.30 a.m. implied that some RIC members started a fire there. A private in the Royal Army Medical Corps was in his ambulance at Dillon's Cross at 9.45 p.m. when he saw some Auxiliaries take some meat from the butcher's shop at Dillon's Cross. The Auxiliaries, who were drunk, put it in his ambulance and threatened to shoot him unless he took the meat back to barracks. A private in the Royal Army Service Corps, who was with an ambulance at Dillon's Cross treating wounded Auxiliary policemen at 9 p.m., 'actually saw Auxiliary Police setting fire to houses'. A quartermaster sergeant in the South Staffordshire Regiment, gave evidence of drunken civilians and drunken firemen.

The last witnesses seem to be concerned to remove any blame for the events of the night from their soldiers. A lance sergeant in the 2nd Hampshire Regiment, who was responsible for collating any absentees from the regiment at 10 p.m. reported that there were no absentees at that hour. An orderly sergeant of the 2nd South Staffordshire Regiment said that reveille roll call showed only one man absent. A Royal Engineers sergeant stated that 33 Company of the RE were all present at tattoo roll call. A Royal Army Service Corps sergeant stated that the 1155 Company of the RASC Mechanical Transport was present at tattoo roll call, and the final witness stated that the 6th Armoured Car Company was also present at roll call at 10.30 p.m.

In its conclusions the court of enquiry decided that it could not point the finger at any individual, but came to the opinion 'that the outrages in Cork City were organised and carried out by the Auxiliary Police … and that certain members of the RIC assisted them … and that no evidence has been produced to connect a soldier with any of these outrages but on the contrary the evidence indicates that the soldiers did their utmost to stop them.' In reality, however, the evidence seems to reflect rather a lack of positive action on the part of the military and a certain sense that they may have been afraid of provoking the Auxiliaries.

# APPENDIX 2

# THE STRICKLAND ENQUIRY

On 16 December 1920 the official military court of enquiry began, by order of Major General Strickland, and over five days took statements from thirty-eight witnesses, including re-examining some of the earlier witnesses from the Higginson Enquiry. A request had been made that a senior police officer should sit on the panel of the enquiry, the final composition of which was three military officers, one district inspector from the RIC and a legal advisor. Five RIC men, six Auxiliaries, nine civilians and eighteen soldiers gave statements, and proceedings were closed to the press, so that the evidence heard could not be reported on and the identities of the witnesses would not be disclosed. Although summoned, the lord mayor of Cork did not attend.

Some of the most interesting eyewitness statements are reproduced below.

## George Willen, ex-soldier

*A statement by a civilian ex-soldier living at Dillon's Cross*

At about 19.30 hours on December 11, I heard two or three bombs explode. Shortly afterwards the house door was opened and I was told to put my hands up. The man who told me to put my hands up was about 5ft 10ins in height wearing a British warm coat and tam-o-shanter cap. He had a queer sort of a flat nose. I could identify him. In addition I saw two men behind him; one was wearing a black, stiff RIC cap and another in soldiers' uniform with three medals. He had two badges on his left arm. They were all armed with revolvers. They told me to get the furniture out of the house as they were going to burn it. This I did and they assisted me in doing so.

After depositing the furniture in the road, one went and brought some petrol, the petrol was in a square tin. They sprinkled petrol over the furniture and set it alight. They went in to the back yard and got some thirty chickens, wrung their necks and threw them on the fire. I spent the night in the field with my wife. At 6.30 the next morning, I returned to the house and found the man with the black RIC cap still there. He told me to get off the street and stay in my house, which I did.

## Observations made by Pastor Fred W. Gracey on the night of Saturday–Sunday, 11–12 last

Returning from a sick call at 10 p.m. I came by way of Patrick Street, and was warned by some civilians, when I reached Woolworth's, that the Black and Tans were at Patrick Bridge, and that I should not go that way. I went on however, knowing that I had a permit and should have nothing to fear. As I turned the bend of the street, I saw a group of men at Evan's shop, and as I came to Dowden's shop, these men stopped me and shouted 'hands up'. I obeyed the order, and when they came to where I stood they were most menacing. There were three or four of them, and at least one was dressed in civilian clothes. They all brandished revolvers, which were held (two of them) against my body, while they swore in a most excited manner and when I told them that I was a Baptist minister that seemed to be no help to them. I said that I had a permit, which they allowed me to produce, and then having read same they became apologetic and explained, 'There was an ambush tonight, Sir and that is why we are on the streets now' and they told me I should hurry off. And [they] fired in the air after I had gone. They returned to Evan's corner, and immediately breaking glass attracted my attention, and as I looked back I could see them smashing the windows of Evan's shop.

When I got to Patrick's Bridge there was another group of the same kind of men, at the Standard House corner, and a tramcar was drawn up there, and some loud altercation was taking place with the motor-man and conductor and some civilians. I did not delay to see what it was, but turned into this house. On going to the front windows some little time after I saw this tramcar at the Mathew statue and ablaze. While watching this, my attention was drawn to a conflagration away to the right, which afterwards proved to be the fire at Grant's. Then, between 11 and

12 o'clock other fires more to the left of my view started up. While watching these, I saw a number of men, whom I judge to be some of the same group I had seen earlier, some of them in long black coats with tam-o-shanter caps, coming to the premises of Mangan's the jewellers. They struck at the roller screens, and in a very few minutes had succeeded in rolling the screens up from the windows on either side of the doorway. Several shots were fired through the glass, and the loud sound of smashing glass was heard.

They then made their way into the shop and further sounds of breaking glass could be heard. They went away up Patrick Street again, and after some little time seemed to return again bearing suitcases and some bags. Going into Mangan's they emerged later, each carrying a bag in each hand, which by the manner they were carried seemed to be heavily filled. They proceeded over Patrick's Bridge in the direction of Bridge Street, and I heard one voice call out something about the 'Soldier's home'. All this could be clearly seen from my window as the blazing tramcar was right opposite Mangan's shop and besides, at this time I was using binoculars. I tried to disabuse my mind of the impression that these were some of His Majesty's Forces, but this closer examination only confirmed this, although there were one or two in civilian clothes among them.

On more than one occasion the curfew troops in lorries passed by these men at the open Mangan's shop, taking no notice apparently of them, but on a third occasion I heard an exchange of words between the lorry and the men around the looted and destroyed shop, and then the lorry passed. Between 11 and 12 o'clock that night a lorry full of Auxiliaries passed down Camden Quay firing indiscriminately. Two bullets entered two windows of this house.

My sole reason for making these observations known, is in order to help the military authorities to know some of the facts. As an officiating minister of the forces, I feel that no good can come to the men or government by covering this up. There is unbounded sympathy with the men in the appalling provocation being given them continually, but their lawless actions cannot be denied on this occasion.

Signed Fred W. Gracey

17th December 1920.

A burnt-out tram near the Fr Mathew statue on Patrick Street. According to an Irish Labour Party eyewitness, 'I noticed a flame of fire in the street, and looking out I saw a tramcar in flames near Father Matthew [*sic*] Statue.' (Courtesy of University College Dublin Archives, UCDA P80/PH/17)

## Mr Stephen Powell of 3 & 4 Patrick Street

I am Managing Director of James Mangan's Jewellers and Goldsmiths, occupiers of No. 3 & 4 Patrick Street. At about 21.00 hours on December 11th I returned from a short walk with my wife, the streets were very quiet, and I had an apprehension that something unpleasant was about to happen. I remained in the shop and my wife went upstairs. I did some clerical work. As shots were being fired in the neighbourhood my wife said 'Come upstairs.' This was between 21.00 and 22.00 hours. My nephew and myself went upstairs as my wife was already upstairs. My nephew, at about 22.05 hours left the room to get a drink of water. He came back and said, 'There is a tramcar on fire outside.' I went to see it. I saw well up Patrick Street the glare of another fire, which I thought was on the top of Patrick Street. I watched the tramcar burning for about a quarter of an hour. I then went to the back of the house to see if I could see any fires in the south part of the city, I saw none. Overhearing voices at the back of the house I looked out and saw my neighbour at No. 1, getting out at the back of his premises and walking on to the roof. I listened to ascertain the cause. My nephew who was at the back of the house, returned and said, 'Some men are looking up at the building.' One of them said, 'This is Mangan's.'

My nephew said, 'You had better come to the front.' I went almost immediately and I saw that the step ladder which I had placed between the shop door and the shutter door as a barricade, lying in the street. I said, 'They are in.' I rushed downstairs and switched on one electric light and saw the form of an individual, whom I took to be a British officer looking towards me through the broken inner shop door. I rushed across the shop and shouted 'Alright.' He said 'Open up.' The door was jammed owing to the broken glass which had fallen on the mat. I pushed it away with my foot. He walked in and said to me, 'Your keys.' I said, 'I will get them for you, but do not alarm my wife she is nervous.' I went upstairs and joined my wife, and we all went on to the garden roof. In my mind there was a possibility of us being burnt. During this time I went quietly part of the way downstairs. Half an hour or three-quarter after they entered I heard them walking up the workshop stairs of the firm in the next house. I said, 'They are after me for the keys.' I said, 'They will come up this side presently.' Ten minutes later they came up the residential stairs – I met them. The leader said, 'This way Tom.' I will not definitely swear it was Tom, but it was an abbreviated Christian name. The first to meet me was a tall man who demanded the keys. 'Your keys,' he said. I replied, 'I will get them for you.'

He and two others followed us into the bedroom. I said, 'We are Loyalists.' I went down myself leading the way into the strong room. I opened the strong room door and turned on the light. I left the strong room by the small stairs leading to it and came back in to the shop. After getting back to the shop I saw every man there with different articles. One man in an officer's dress had silver soup ladles. He said,

'I can make use of these.' One man in civilian clothes with a grey suit – gentlemanly appearance – he had apparently just finished clearing a case. I then turned around and said, 'Will you please tell me when you have done, so that I can close the shop and save it from others.' I then went back upstairs. In about a quarter of an hour an explosion occurred down below. Finally at the end of half an hour the marauding party consisting of about ten, left. The leader was a tall man dressed as a British officer. I do not remember if he wore a Sam Browne belt – but I do remember that he was not wearing a great coat. He was wearing medal ribbons, I think two rows. He was a man of about forty years of age, pale but I do not remember anything else about him. Of the others, one at least was dressed something like an RIC constable but too small in stature that is the generally accepted standard of the RIC. He had no hat on but a handkerchief around his mouth. Two or three were dressed in khaki with khaki tam o' shanters. Of the remainder, one at least was dressed as a British officer, and the rest in various uniforms. After about half an hour I eventually came down and found the shop in the possession of two soldiers in steel helmets, also a constabulary man. They said to me 'You are all right, we have been placed on guard here and will admit nobody.'

I found the following articles in my shop:–

A new civilian coat with Cash & Co. marked on it

An electric hand torch

Portion of a bomb

One tin of petrol

Regimental button

A white handkerchief

Lady's Limerick lace collar

Lady's golf jacket

and several other articles which I will hand to the court. My wife and nephew can corroborate as much of the above evidence as effects [*sic*] them. The two men I heard spoke with an English accent.

Signed

Stephen Powell

AT THE SIGN OF

# THE PILLAR CLOCK

(Opposite Father Mathew Statue, in Patrick Street)

IS THE OLD-ESTABLISHED FIRM OF

# JAMES MANGAN, Ltd.,

## Celebrated for Souvenir Jewellery.

Before leaving Cork, Visitors are respectfully invited to inspect the

### LARGE AND VARIED STOCK.

Beautiful Designs in Gold and Silver Brooches, Bangles, Scarf Pins, Pendants, Charms, Belt Clasps, Paper Knives, Candlesticks, Photo Frames, Ink Stands, Vases, Button Hooks, etc., all Mounted with Irish Marble. :: :: 40 patterns of Souvenir Spoons. :: ::

# JAMES MANGAN, Ltd.,

3, PATRICK STREET, CORK ( Near the Bridge ).

Spectacle Specialists, Watchmakers, Jewellers.

*Makers of the Celebrated Clock in Shandon Steeple, CORK.*

Over 1,000 Articles, with the City Arms, in Enamel, from 10d. to £1. Large Assortment of Bog Oak Ornaments.

James Mangan Ltd was the finest clockmaker in Cork and installed the four clocks in the tower of Shandon. The shop would have contained much valuable merchandise making it an obvious choice for looters. (Author's collection)

## Mrs Louise Gaffney of The Munster Arcade Cork

On December 11th, owing to the disturbances of the previous day and disturbed night, I retired to bed early, about 21.00 hours. There had been shooting in the streets going on prior to this during the evening. At about 22.00 hours one of my maids reported a fire at Grant's shop. I put on a coat over my night attire and went into the maid's room overlooking Elbow Lane. At about 23.30 hours one of my men came in and said that he had heard some men outside threaten to burn the Munster Arcade next. Shortly afterwards this proved to be true. I then said, 'We must leave the house' and took my people with me towards the private door in Elbow Lane. As we approached the door, they fired up at the window. My man called out 'There are women here.' The reply was 'The women are safe, but we do not know what we will do with you.' We got down to the door. On arriving at the door we found that it had been burst open. Standing at the right of it there was a man in khaki whom I took to be an officer. He had a muffler around his face. He was wearing a British warm coat and a service dress hat. On the left of the door was standing another man dressed in khaki and a black Balmoral hat. We passed out and were then told to march on and then to halt. On coming through the archway we saw eight other men in uniform. Of these eight men, one appeared to be dressed as an officer in khaki with a service dress hat. He was carrying two heavily loaded bags. I also noticed a Highlander. He had an overcoat on, but I distinguished the kilt as he went upstairs. Two of them seemed to be Black and Tans. They passed me and went upstairs. At the end of Elbow Lane I saw another man in uniform who was marching up and down. He was dressed all in black. I asked him if I could go back and get some clothes. He replied 'Madam you did not consider us, we will not consider you.' He spoke with a North of Ireland accent. This man summoned another dressed in plain clothes, and was asked if he could recognise any of us. He shook his head. We were then told we could go. A small bunty man put a pistol to my face and said we could go. Shots were fired after us. In Georges Street we saw a number of men standing about; I think they were Black and Tans. Then we saw a number of men moving down Morgan Street carrying trunks and bundles. Some of these men had black caps and some had tam-o-shanters. We finally got to a restaurant in Marlboro Street where we stayed for the night. The man with the loot fired six shots after us. I myself was nearly shot in the heel. I describe these men as Black and Tans because the boy told me they were. My servant Miss Kathleen Murphy can corroborate as much of my above evidence as effects [*sic*] her. She was present with me at the time.

Signed

Louise Maria Gaffney

The ruins of Egan's jewellers, Sunner's Chemist and The Munster Arcade. (Author's collection)

## Statement of Sergeant James Pearce, 2nd Hampshire Regiment

I was Sergeant in charge of the main gate from 10.00 hours on 11 December to 10.00 on 12 December. Just before 20.00 hrs on 11 December a cadet ran into barracks stating that there had been an ambush down the road and wanted to turn my guard out. I refused. From then until 22.00 hours, I noticed men of the Auxiliary police coming out and going in to the barracks continually, singly and in small parties. They did not appear to be controlled. I saw rifles and revolvers on them. At about 22.00 hours about 30 of them left together, they were in a mob, not formed. From 22.45 hours until 01.30 hours on the 12th Dec, men of the Auxiliary police were coming back into the barracks singly and in pairs – some were the worse for drink. Every man was carrying something which appeared to be loot, some were carrying bundles and some were carrying dressing cases. At 01.30 I was relieved of responsibility of the gate by an officer and a party of the South Staffordshire Regt. The people I took to be Auxiliary police were some in mufti; I cannot say the number, some in uniform, with black overcoats, and some with trench coats. Some in uniform were wearing the tam o'shanter hats and some civilian caps.

No absentee report was sent around that night from units in the barracks. I saw an Auxiliary police Garford [a type of armoured military vehicle] going in and out of the barracks with Auxiliary policemen on board, between 20.00 and 23.00 hours. At 23.30 hours the Garford left the barracks and I did not see it return again. I resumed charge of the gate at 06.15 on the 12th Dec. and handed over charge to the garrison police at 07.00 hours. Two soldiers were placed in my guardroom on a charge of highway robbery at about 21.30 on the 11th Dec. These men were not on duty. At 03.15 and 03.30 hours two soldiers on duty were confined to my guardroom on a charge of drunkenness. At 01.30 on the 12th I had orders to search the men coming in, but nobody came in between that time and the time that I handed the gate over to the officer of the Staffordshire Regt. During my tour of duty and after 22.00 hours on the 11th I saw no man of the Cameron Highlanders come into the barracks. I have nothing to do with the control of the Auxiliary Police.

## The Strickland Report

At the time this enquiry was seen as a sham by the citizens of Cork, part of a larger attempt by the British authorities to cover up what had happened. However, in an interesting turn of events, when the final report of the enquiry finally became available in 1999, its findings are highly critical of the Auxiliaries in particular and also of the chain of command. This may explain why the report was not released in 1920.

It is worth recording this report here in full:

1) The court has taken the evidence of 38 witnesses (Military, Police and Civilians).

Notices to attend the Court of Enquiry were issued against the following.

The Lord Mayor of Cork.
J. J. Walsh, Esq., M.P. for Cork City.
W. Roche Esq., M.P. for Cork City (who styles himself Liam De Roiste Esq., M.P. for Cork City).

The attendance of the two first named could not be enforced as their whereabouts are unknown.

The latter declined, and was escorted to the court by an escort, but he declined to give evidence.

The City Engineer was also warned to attend but his council refused to allow him to do so.

2) On the night of Dec. 11th there was an Ambush of a party of the Auxiliary Division R.I.C. at Dillon's Cross, within 200 yards of Victoria Barracks, Cork. This Ambush was laid by the Rebels and resulted in the following casualties – thirteen wounded, of which one subsequently died.

This ambush in the opinion of the court led up to the subsequent deplorable events of the night in question.

3) The Court having considered the evidence are of the opinion both from the evidence of intention and from the evidence as to facts, both direct and circumstantial, that the fires at the premises of Messrs. Grant & Co. and Messrs. Cash & Co. and at the Munster Arcade, and also the burning of bicycles outside the Republican Bicycle Shop were caused by the men of 'K' Company of the Auxiliary Division R.I.C.

The Court are of the opinion that circumstantial, but not conclusive evidence exists that three members of the R.I.C. were implicated in the fire at the City Hall. The destruction by fire of other premises is all attributable to the spread of the conflagration from the primary outbreaks. The extent of the subsequent destruction is considered to be largely due to the inadequacy of the Local Fire Brigade both in personnel and material.

4) Numerous cases of looting are proved in evidence of which the most serious can be traced to men of the Auxiliary Police.

Though the evidence on the point is not conclusive, the Court are of opinion that the ring-leaders in these acts of crime were Temporary Constables (of whom a small establishment is attached to each Company of Cadets), masquerading in such a way as to appear, to the inexperienced, as officers.

There is evidence that a small number of R.I.C., who, the Court consider, were recruits, was implicated in the looting. There is also evidence of a soldier in Highland dress being in the company of the marauders.

In the back streets, and at later periods of the events it is clear from the evidence that Civilians were concerned in the looting and consumption of liquor, and in individual acts of theft.

5) The firing of arms without cause, and other lawless behaviour has been proved against ten of the Auxiliary Police, while earlier in the night a few shots were fired by Rebel forces.

In another part of the town and before 10 p.m. two soldiers were arrested on a charge of Highway Robbery. All crime committed during the night was against property, and except terrorism, there was no crime against the person.

6) The necessary self-restraint to withstand such a strain upon the human passions as that imposed by the outrage at Dillon's Cross can only be imparted by discipline.

From the evidence that is adduced, the court does not consider that discipline of an adequate standard existed in this Company of Auxiliary Police. Discipline can only be inculcated by training, the infliction of penalties, and the personality of the Commanders; in respect of this particular unit opportunities for the first were lacking, and the powers of punishment vested in the Commander were inadequate, whilst the personalities of the Officers, however dominating could not possibly produce the required effect in the very short period during which these Officers had been associated with their men. Whilst holding the Commanding Officer to blame for not living with and constantly associating himself with his Command, the Court consider that the higher authority who ordered a unit in so raw a state to an area where active operations might be expected, must be held very largely responsible for the subsequent happenings.

7) It is considered that the disposition and strength of the troops were appropriate to deal with any situation that was likely to arise in Cork on the night in question.

The Military and Regular Police performed their duties efficiently.

An outbreak on the scale in question, in view moreover of the fact that the Company of the Auxiliary Police left Barracks under their own Officers, presented the greatest difficulties to the Military Officers concerned, in as much as not only had they to consider the possibilities of Rebel action, but because also it must necessarily take some time for them to realize that the majority of the Company of the Auxiliary Police had broken from the control of their own Officers. The situation was unparalleled, Martial Law was not in force; and the alternative of employing armed force by the Military against an armed Auxiliary force of Police would have resulted in a conflict.

8) In view of the conduct of the majority of the Company of the Auxiliary

Division, a tribute is due to those others who resisted temptation and stood by their own Officers.

9) For your information a Map of the area concerned is attached.

Signed at Victoria Barracks, Cork, this 21st day of December 1920.

## A Report by the RIC Officer on the Strickland Enquiry

In an interesting turn of events, the RIC district inspector who sat on the panel during the Strickland Enquiry took exception to some of the conclusions drawn and submitted the following minority report, which in turn led to a rebuff by the president of the enquiry.

## Military Enquiry as to the Burnings in Cork on the night of 11th and 12th December 1920.

With reference to the above enquiry I regret to say that I am not in agreement with all the findings of the court. The enquiry opened at Victoria Barracks on 16th inst. I did not join it as a member until 18th inst. There were eleven witnesses examined during the 16th and 17th inst. The rules of evidence were not observed during my time as a member of the court. I am not satisfied with any evidence that I have heard or read that there was any incendiarism or looting by members of the R.I.Constabulary.

A witness named Jervois stated emphatically that he took five bottles of whiskey from an R.I.C. man who was wearing his Great Coat. He stated that the R.I.C. man had the bottles in his pockets, and that there were two quart bottles and three ordinary liquor bottles. Jervois further states that from the R.I.C. man he took several armfuls of underclothing from under his Great Coat. All the R.I.C. in Cork in the night in question have been fully accounted for by their officers who were examined and who were prepared to produce further evidence if required.

Owing to the conditions under which K. Co. Auxiliary Division of the R.I.C. had to live in Victoria Barracks, Cork, it seemed impossible for Lt. Col. Latimer, their C.O., to properly or adequately associate with his command, and I think it rather hard to censure him on the matter. I cannot, under any circumstances, agree to any censure being meted out to the High Authority who, as the finding points out, ordered a unit in so raw a state to an area where active operations might be expected.

21/12/1920     D.I. James Deignan

## Supplementary

The remainder of the court have read the above statement of District Inspector Deignan but are unable to in any way alter or amend their opinion as already expressed. …

They also desire to put on record that a copy of the evidence of the 11 witnesses referred to was handed to District Inspector Deignan and he was given opportunity to have recalled any such witnesses as he desired, but he did not take advantage thereof.

21/12/1920     President (Lt Colonel Stapleton)

Children gather outside the still smoking ruins of the
Lee Boot Company premises. (Author's collection)

RUINS OF LONDON HOUSE, LEE BOOT CO. & SCULLY & O'CONN

# BIBLIOGRAPHY

Abbott, Richard, *Police Casualties in Ireland 1919–1922* (Mercier Press, 2000)

Anon, *The Burning of Cork City. A Tale of Arson, Loot and Murder* (South Gate Books, 1978)

Barry, Tom, *Guerilla Days in Ireland* (Mercier Press, 2013)

— *The Reality of the Anglo Irish War 1920–21 in West Cork Refutations, Corrections and Comments on Liam Deasy's Towards Ireland Free* (Anvil Books, 1974)

Bennett, Richard, *The Black & Tans* (Edward Hulton, 1959)

Borgonovo, John (ed.), *Florence and Josephine O'Donoghue's War of Independence: A Destiny That Shapes Our Ends* (Irish Academic Press, 2006)

— *Spies, Informers and the 'Anti-Sinn Féin Society': The Intelligence War in Cork City 1920–1921* (Irish Academic Press, 2007)

Breen, Daniel and Spalding, Tom, *The Cork International Exhibition 1902–1903: A Snapshot of Edwardian Cork* (Irish Academic Press, 2014)

Chavasse, Moirin, *Terence MacSwiney* (Clonmore and Reynolds, 1961)

Costello, Francis J., *Enduring the Most: the Life and Death of Terence MacSwiney* (Brandon Books, 1995)

Crowley, J., Ó Drisceoil, D. and Murphy, M. (eds), *Atlas of the Irish Revolution* (Cork University Press, 2017)

Crozier, Brigadier General Frank Percy, *Ireland For Ever* (Cedric Chivers Ltd, 1971)

Deasy, Liam, *Towards Ireland Free: The West Cork Brigade in the War of Independence 1917–1921* (Mercier Press, 1973)

Hart, Peter, *The I.R.A. and Its Enemies: Violence and Community in Cork 1916–1923* (Oxford University Press, 1999)

Harvey, Dan and White, Gerry, *The Barracks: A History of Victoria/Collins Barracks, Cork* (Mercier Press, 1997)

Healy, James N., *The Story of Roches Stores* (Litho Press, 1981)

Herlihy, Jim, *The Royal Irish Constabulary: A Complete Alphabetical List of Officers and Men, 1816–1922* (Four Courts Press, 1999)

— *The Royal Constabulary: A Short History and Genealogical Guide with a Select List of Medal Awards and Casualties* (Four Courts Press, 1997)

Herlihy, Roger, *A Walk through the South Parish: "Where Cork Began"* (Red Abbey Publications, 2010)

Leland, Mary, *Dwyers of Cork: A Family Business and a Business Family* (Ted Dwyer, 2008)

Lenihan, Michael, *Hidden Cork: Charmers, Chancers and Cute Hoors* (Mercier Press, 2009)

— *Pure Cork* (Mercier Press, 2011)

— *Timeless Cork* (Mercier Press, 2013)

Mac Curtain, Fionnula, *Remember ... it's for Ireland: A Family Memoir of Tomás Mac Curtáin* (Mercier Press, 2006)

McCall Ernest, *The Auxiliaries, Tudor's Toughs. A Study of the Auxiliary Division Royal Irish Constabulary 1920–1922* (Red Coat Publishing, 2010)

— *The Auxies: A Pictorial History of the Auxiliary Division Royal Irish Constabulary 1920–1922* (Red Coat Publishing, 2013)

McCarthy, Thomas, *Rising from the Ashes: The Burning of Cork's Carnegie Library and the Rebuilding of Its Collections* (Cork City Council Libraries, 2010)

McGonagle, Helen, *A Room of their Own: Cork Carnegie Free Library & its Ladies Reading Room 1905–1915* (Cork City Council Libraries, 2015)

McSwiney, Joe, *The Golden Age of Cork Cinemas* (Rose Arch Publications, 2013)

Neeson, Geraldine, *In My Mind's Eye: The Cork I Knew and Loved* (Prestige Books, 2001)

Nyhan, Miriam, *Are You Still Below? The Ford Marina Plant, Cork, 1917–1984* (Collins Press, 2007)

O'Callaghan, Antóin, *The Lord Mayors of Cork* (Litho Press, 2000)

— *Cork's St Patrick's Street: A History* (Collins Press, 2010)

O'Donoghue, Florence, *Tomás MacCurtain* (Anvil Books, 1959)

Ó Drisceoil, Diarmuid and Ó Drisceoil, Donal, *Serving a City: The Story of Cork's English Market* (Collins Press, 2011)

— *Beamish & Crawford: The History of an Irish Brewery* (Collins Press, 2015)

Ó Ruairc, Pádraig Óg, *Revolution: A Photographic History of Revolutionary Ireland 1913–1923* (Mercier Press, 2011)

Poland, Pat, *'Fire call': Cork Fire Brigade Centenary Review 1877–1977* (Society of St Florian, 1977)

— *For Whom the Bells Tolled: A History of the Cork Fire Service 1622–1900* (History Press Ireland, 2010)

Quinlivan, Aodh, *Philip Monahan: A Man Apart. The Life and Times of Ireland's First Local Authority Manager* (Institute of Public Administration, 2006)

— *Dissolved. The Remarkable Story of How Cork Lost its Corporation in 1924* (Cork City Council Libraries, 2017)

Roynane, Liam and Mullins, John, *A Grand Parade: Memories of Cork City Libraries 1855–2005* (Cork City Council Libraries, 2005)

Ruiséal, Liam, *Liam Ruiséal Remembers* (Tower Books, 1978)

— 'Some Activities in Cork City 1920–1921', *Capuchin Annual* 1970

Ryan, Meda, *Tom Barry: IRA Freedom Fighter* (Mercier Press, 2003)

Spalding, Tom, *A Guide to Cork's Twentieth Century Architecture* (Cork Architectural Press, 2010)

— *Layers: The Design History and Meaning of Public Street Signage in Cork and Other Irish Cities* (Associated Editions, 2013)

Various, *Rebel Cork's Fighting Story 1916–1921: Told by the Men Who Made It* (Anvil Books, 1949)

White, Gerry and O'Shea, Brendan, *Baptised in Blood: The Formation of the Cork Brigade of Irish Volunteers 1913–1916* (Mercier Press, 2005)

— *The Burning of Cork* (Mercier Press, 2006)

Whyte, Louis, *The White Heather Glen: The Kilmichael Story of Grief and Glory* (The Kilmichael and Crossbarry Commemoration Committee, 1995)

## Brochures

O'Donoghue, Florence, 'Two Patriot Priests of Ireland: A Short Biographical Brochure of Fathers Albert and Dominic', 1959

Tír na n-Óg, 'Irish Industries Fair in the City Hall Cork 2nd April to 3rd May 1919'

## Magazine

*St Angela's magazine*, May 1921

## Directories

*Guy's Cork Directory & Almanac*, 1918, 1919, 1920 and 1921

## Reports

*American Commission on the Conditions in Ireland Interim Report* (Hardin and Moore, 1921)

*American Commission on the Conditions in Ireland. Evidence on Conditions in Ireland* (Washington D.C., 1921)

Cutler, Henry, *Report on the Present Condition of the Municipal Buildings* (Guy & Co., 1897)

Irish Labour and Trade Union Congress Dublin, *Who Burnt Cork City?* (1921)

*Report of the British Labour Commission to Ireland and London 1921*

*Report of the City Engineer Concerning the Conflagration in the City on 11th & 12th December 1920*

*Report of the Higginson Enquiry*

*Report of the Strickland Enquiry*

*RIC Minority Report*

## Newspapers

*Cork Examiner, The*

*Evening Echo*

*Cork Constitution*

*Cork Holy Bough*

*Skibbereen Eagle, The*
*Weekly Examiner*
*Weekly Examiner and Weekly Herald Christmas Supplement 1920*

## Websites
The Auxiliary Division of the Royal Irish Constabulary: www.theauxiliaries.com
Cork Past and Present: www.corkpastandpresent.ie
House of Commons historical records for the 1920s: https://api.parliament.uk/historic-hansard/sittings/C20
The National Archives, Kew: www.nationalarchives.gov.uk

A busy scene on Patrick Street, pre-burning. (Author's collection)

# INDEX

## A

Albert Quay 86
Alexander Grant & Co. 33, 46, 47, 106, 108–110, 113, 131, 147, 148, 184, 187, 189, 200, 201, 202, 203, 204, 225, 230, 236, 240
Allman & Co. 34, 35, 39
American Commission on Conditions in Ireland 53, 74, 76, 84, 86, 141, 167, 182, 183
American Shoe Co. 23, 78, 81, 200, 201
Arnott, Sir John 33
Artane Clothing Company 22, 80
Auxiliary Division 11–13, 16, 20, 21, 23, 41, 53, 55–59, 64, 68, 82, 91–93, 95, 96, 98, 106, 114, 115, 121, 123, 125, 131, 143, 159, 160, 165, 172, 173, 175, 179, 180, 188, 191, 219–229, 231, 238–241, 243

## B

Bachelor's Quay 84
Balbriggan 53
Ballyhooly Road 226
Ballyknockane 62
Ballymakeera 91
Barrack Street 21, 114
Barriscalle's jewellers 81
Barry, Patrick 186–188
Barry, Tadhg 62, 180
Barry, Tom 12, 90–92, 180
Beamish & Crawford 89
Black and Tans 11, 16, 19–21, 41, 52, 53, 55, 56, 59, 64, 68, 75, 82, 106, 115, 123, 159, 160, 165, 172, 173, 230, 236, 237
Blackpool 62, 116

Blackrock 20, 22, 32, 81
Blackthorn House 23, 81
Blemens, Frederick 81
Blemens, James 81
Bowling Green Street 181
Brian Dillon's house 94, 96, 97
Bridge Street 81, 184, 231
British Labour Party 172, 221
Brixton Prison 70
Broad Lane 21
Broadmoor Criminal Lunatic Asylum 219
Brooke Hughes 55, 107, 146
Burnford National School 62
Burton Ltd 146, 159, 163, 164, 187, 200, 201

## C

Cahill & Co. 23, 81
Camden Quay 23, 66, 81, 82, 231
Cameron Highlanders 56, 238
Carmichael's 33
Carnegie, Andrew 137
Carnegie Free Library 49, 106, 109, 116, 136–139, 157, 171, 174, 183, 191, 212, 213
Cash & Co. 27, 29, 32, 34, 39, 106, 109, 113, 123, 127, 146, 147, 150, 159, 163, 184, 187, 191, 199, 200, 203, 205, 225, 226, 234, 240
Cashman & Co. 151, 184
Castle & Co. 21
Castle Street 33, 39
Castletownkenneigh 91
Centre Park Road 167
Chapman, Spencer 96, 219
Chave, Constable 21
Chillingworth & Levie 198, 199, 201, 203

Churchill, Winston 11, 176

City Hall 12, 13, 17, 18, 20–23, 49, 66, 70–74, 77, 80, 81, 84–87, 106, 116, 133, 135, 137, 170, 171, 174, 183, 191, 192, 212, 213, 215, 221, 240

Clogher 91

Cobh (Queenstown) 71

Cohalan, Bishop Daniel 13, 19, 61, 178–181

Collins, Michael 71

Commons Road 20

Cook Street 22, 24, 121, 147, 151, 184, 198, 199

Cooke, F. 65

Coppeen 91

Cork Arcade 21

Cork Corporation 13, 25, 32, 54, 62, 74, 77, 86, 140, 145, 175, 179, 183, 185, 188, 197–203, 213, 215, 217

Cork Examiner, The 17, 26, 79, 95, 96, 145, 172, 175, 179–181, 188, 189, 213

Cork Exhibition, 1852 22

Cork Exhibition, 1902–3 42, 85

Cork Furniture Stores 38, 152, 184

Cork Gaol 20, 70

Cork No. 1 Brigade 62, 81

Cork Progressive Association 213

Cornmarket yard 61

Coyle, Albert 76

Crake, Francis 93

Crowley, Timothy 219

Crozier, Frank Percy 21, 53, 56, 58, 220, 221

Cudmore's fruiter 146, 163, 200, 201

Cummins & Co. 151, 152

D

Dáil Éireann 51, 54

Dalton's restaurant 12, 23, 81

Daly, John 113, 200

Dartry Dye Co. 127

Day's 32

De Róiste, Liam 239

Deasy, Liam 180

Deasy, Pat 92

Deignan, James 242, 243

Delany, Cornelius 23, 98, 99, 101, 102

Delany, Daniel 98

Delany, Jeremiah 23, 98–101

Delaney, J. F. 110, 117, 145, 239

Dennehy's Cross 20

Dillon's Cross 11, 12, 23, 56, 95, 96, 98, 100, 105, 110, 172, 173, 179, 219, 227, 229, 239, 241

Douglas 32, 81

Dowling, Tom 80

Dublin 11, 50, 61, 71, 115, 116, 214, 215, 221

Dublin Castle 55

Dublin Fire Brigade 115, 139, 140, 141

Dublin Hill 98, 102

Dunlea, William 99

Dunmanway 91, 179, 180, 219, 220

Dwyer & Co. 21, 68, 80

E

Easter Rising 11, 51, 61, 62, 71, 116

Eastwood, Major F. R. 113, 114

Egan's jewellers. See William Egan & Sons jewellers

Egan, William 39

Elbow Lane 184, 187, 236

Empress Place 20, 226

English Market 12, 109

F

Fair Hill 213

Ferguson Smyth, Gerald Brice 20, 79

Fianna Fáil 68

Fitzgerald, Michael 71
Fitzgerald, Patrick 34, 158, 189, 194, 196, 203
Fitzgerald's menswear 33, 196, 213
Fitzgerald's Park 213
Ford, Henry 10, 159, 167
Forde, Lieutenant H. F. 93
Forrest & Sons 22, 24, 26, 47, 81, 83, 123, 146, 184, 198, 199
French, Sean 191, 213
Fr Mathew Quay 23, 81
Frongoch Internment Camp 61, 62

## G

Gaelic Athletic Association (GAA) 12, 22
Gaelic League 62
Gaffney, Louise Maria 187, 236, 237
Galway city 179
General Post Office (GPO) 79, 109, 225–227
Georges (Oliver Plunkett) Street 12, 106, 151–153, 183, 184, 187, 236
Glanmire 19
Glanmire Road, Lower 20
Glanmire Station 56
Gleann 91
Goggin, Mick 67
Gordon Highlanders 108
Grace, Edward 159, 167
Gracey, Pastor Fred W. 230, 231
Grand Parade 12, 22, 47, 80, 105, 106, 108, 153, 212, 223, 225
Great Georges (Washington) Street 54
Greenwood, Hamar 171, 173, 175, 188, 219, 221, 222
Griffin, Fr Michael 179
Griffith, Arthur 71
Guthrie, Cadet Cecil 93
Guy & Co. 15, 16, 33
Guy's Directory 33, 145, 146

## H

Hackett's jewellers 108, 148
Hampshire Regiment 114, 223–227, 238
Hardwick Street 22, 80
Harrington, Sir Stanley 213
Harrington's Row 98
Haynes & Son 109, 131, 147, 148, 164, 184, 201
Healy, Maurice 175
Higginson, Brigadier General Harold Whitla 175, 220, 223
Higginson Enquiry 175, 223–229
Hill, Henry 203, 205
Hilser Brothers 105, 115
Hudson, Captain P. H. 114
Hutson, Alfred 12, 86, 88, 108, 111, 113, 137, 140, 185

## I

Imperial Hotel 56
Inchigeela 93
Irish Labour Party report 16, 17, 99, 106, 115, 118, 121, 123, 125, 127, 128, 131, 147, 171, 173, 191, 218, 219, 232
Irish Republican Army (IRA) 11–13, 19, 21, 51, 53, 54, 56, 61–63, 67, 68, 70, 79, 91–93, 95, 96, 98, 100, 178, 180
Irish Republican Brotherhood 62
Irish Transport and General Workers' Union (ITGWU) 12, 23, 81, 82
Irish Volunteers 11, 19, 51, 54, 61, 62, 68, 71

## J

James Mangan Ltd 33, 41, 115, 187, 224, 225, 231–233, 235
John Sisk & Son 203, 214, 215
Johnstown 93

John Teape jewellers  23
Jones & Kelly  215

# K

K Company  21, 56, 57, 95, 180, 219–221, 243
Keating, James  38
Kelleher, Thomas  213
Kenworthy, Lieutenant Commander  171, 222
Kilmichael  11, 12, 23, 90–93
King (MacCurtain) Street  21, 23, 81, 115, 158
King Street Barracks  20, 65, 67
Knockcrogherty  53

# L

Latimer, Lieutenant Colonel Owen W. R. G.  21, 56, 219, 220, 222, 243
Lee Boot Company  106, 146, 149, 150, 159, 184, 203, 244
Lee Cinema  35, 141, 147, 150, 184
Lehane, James  91
Limerick Fire Brigade  115
Lloyd George, David  12, 65, 176
London House  33–35, 127, 158, 159, 184, 189, 196, 203, 244

# M

MacCurtain, Elizabeth (née Walsh)  62–65
MacCurtain Street  67, 81, 89, 197
MacCurtain, Tomás  11, 19–21, 60, 62–68, 71, 73, 79, 197
MacNeill, Eoin  11, 61
Macroom  91, 93
Macroom Engineering Co.  201
MacSwiney, Peter  74
MacSwiney, Terence  11, 20, 21, 62, 68–74
Madden, Robert  80
Magahey, William  85

Magner, Canon Thomas J.  179, 180, 219
*Manchester Guardian, The*  13
Mangan's jewellers. *See* James Mangan Ltd
Marina, the  10
Market Lane  108
Marlboro Street  23, 153, 187, 236
Marsh & Sons auctioneers  132
Maylor Street  128, 144, 146, 149, 150, 152, 157, 184, 187, 199, 201
McAuliffe, Finbarr  188
McCabe, James. J.  65
McCarthy, Rev. F.  106
McCarthy, Michael  91, 92
McDonagh, District Inspector  19
McPherson, Ian  65
McSweeney, Fr A.  32
McSweeney, Rev. P.  105
Merchants Quay  116
Merchant Street  38, 40, 108, 145, 149, 152, 159, 164, 184, 193, 194, 196
Mercy Hospital  99, 101, 180
Michael Roche's jewellers  23, 81, 82
Military Foot Police  226
Monahan, Philip  202, 213, 215
Mulcahy, William  84
Municipal School of Commerce  68
Munster Arcade  30, 32, 33, 43, 55, 106, 107, 109, 113, 123, 131, 146, 150–152, 159, 161, 183–188, 210, 236, 237, 240
Murphy Brothers  206
Murphy, Joseph  21, 71
Murphy, Kathleen  237
Murtagh, Joseph  19, 63, 66, 67
Mutton Lane  108, 109, 147

# N

National Bank  143
National Monument  42
New York House  117, 145, 149